Finding Your Way Home

The Missing Manual

Shira Harrison

Dedication

For my sister, Einat, who left us far too soon at 17. You didn't get the chance to heal in this life, but I hope, in some way, this book reaches you wherever you are and brings you the peace you deserve.

I carry you with me every day, and I hope this work offers the kind of healing we both needed.

With love, always.

You sister, Shira.

Contents

Prologue
The Missing Manual to Finding Home

I am not a mental health professional, although, after spending 25 years in therapy—any possible therapy I could find—I sometimes feel like I could be one. My journey has not been a straightforward path; it has been a winding road filled with countless detours, bumps, and obstacles. I've explored everything from traditional talk therapy to cognitive behavioral therapy, from EMDR to Native American ceremonies, and from energy healing to past life regression.

You name it, I've probably tried it.

What I am, however, is a spiritual person who explores mindfulness daily and a certified Quantum Healing Hypnosis Technique (QHHT) practitioner. My practice with QHHT has allowed me to explore the depths of the subconscious mind, helping others—and myself—uncover the root causes of emotional and spiritual challenges and even heal them. Through this work, I've witnessed the profound healing that can occur when we access our higher selves and embrace the journey inward.

I rediscover myself as time goes by, peeling back the layers of conditioning and old wounds to reveal my true self underneath. My life has been a quest to find my home—a journey to heal the deep wounds of a traumatic childhood and to understand the aftereffects that have rippled through my life.

Some days, I still feel far away from home, lost in the chaos of my thoughts, emotions, and old patterns. But unlike before, I now know the path to find it.

I've discovered that home isn't a place, a person, or a destination. Home is a state of being, a feeling of peace, safety, and belonging that comes from within. It's the place where I can take off all my masks, drop my defenses, and simply be myself.

This book is a collection of my findings and observations gathered along my journey. It is my attempt to share what I've learned in a simple, methodical way. As the title suggests, this is the missing manual for finding your way home—again and again—in a repeatable, reliable way. I've broken it down into steps that you can follow, adapt, and make your own. This isn't a one-size-fits-all approach; it's a guide to help you find what works for you based on your unique experiences and needs.

I hope that by sharing my journey, I can help others who feel lost, disconnected, or far away from their true selves. My goal is not to provide all the answers but to offer a map, a set of tools, and a little bit of guidance to help you navigate your own journey home. Whether you are just beginning your journey or have been searching for a long time, I hope this book provides you with the insight, encouragement, and support you need to find your way.

Enjoy the journey home. It's the most important journey you will ever take. Shira.

Chapter 1

Home is Where the Heart Is: Rediscovering Our Path to Inner Sanctuary

Introduction: The Universal Search for Home

Home is a concept that holds different meanings for different people, but at its core, it represents a place of safety, comfort, and belonging—a place where we can be ourselves without fear of judgment or rejection. For many, home is a physical space filled with familiar smells, sounds, and sights. For others, home is a feeling, a sense of peace and security that resides deep within us. No matter how we define it, the essence of home remains the same: it is where we feel most connected, both to ourselves and to something greater, whether that be our family, community, or the divine.

For much of my life, I longed for this sense of home, a place where I could feel truly safe, loved, and accepted. But my experience of "home" was far from this ideal. I grew up in an environment that was anything but safe or comforting. My childhood home was a place of chaos, neglect, and emotional abuse. I learned early on that home was not a place where I could be myself or express my feelings without fear of criticism or rejection. It was a place where I felt fundamentally wrong as if there was something inherently flawed about me.

Despite these early experiences, I never lost the deep-seated longing for a true home. I carried this yearning with me throughout my life, always searching for a place where I could feel at peace, where I could take off all my masks and just be myself. This quest for home has been a driving force in my journey of self-discovery and healing, and it has led me to explore what "home" truly means and how we can find it within ourselves.

In this chapter, we will explore the deeper meaning of "home" and the universal quest to find it. We will look at how the concept of home has been understood throughout history and across cultures, how it is deeply intertwined with our spiritual beliefs, and how modern society has often led us away from our true home within. Through this exploration, I hope to share my journey and the lessons I've learned along the way, inviting you to begin your own journey back to your inner sanctuary.

Home: A Place of Safety, Comfort, and Authenticity

At its most fundamental level, home is a place where we can be our authentic selves. It is where we feel safe, loved, and accepted. As children, we instinctively seek out this sense of home—a place where we can explore, express, and grow without fear of judgment or rejection. This is why children's drawings of home are often filled with warmth and happiness: simple, colorful houses with open doors, smoke rising from chimneys, and family members smiling together. These drawings capture an innate sense of safety, comfort, and unconditional love.

But what happens when home is not a place of safety and comfort? What happens when a home is a place of fear, neglect, or abuse? For many, like myself, home was not a sanctuary but a battleground—a place where we learned to hide our true selves, suppress our feelings, and wear masks to protect ourselves from criticism and rejection. Growing up in such an environment can leave deep scars, creating a sense of disconnection and longing that follows us into adulthood.

Personal Reflection: My Experience of Home

For much of my childhood, I felt like an outsider in my own home. My parents were often critical and emotionally distant, and their love seemed conditional based on whether I met their expectations. I learned early on that it was safer to keep my feelings to myself, to avoid expressing my needs or desires, and to try to be as "good" as possible to avoid conflict or punishment. This environment taught me to wear a mask, to hide my true self, and to believe that I was not worthy of love just as I was.

Despite the pain and confusion of my early years, I never lost my longing for a true home—a place where I could feel safe, loved, and accepted for who I am. This longing became a driving force in my life, leading me on a journey of self-discovery and healing. I sought out therapy, spiritual practices, and self-help methods, always searching for that elusive sense of home. I came to realize that the home I was seeking was not a physical place but a state of being—a sense of inner peace, belonging, and self-acceptance.

The Historical Perspective: A Longing for Connection

The concept of home has always been central to human life, but its meaning has evolved over time. In the earliest human civilizations, the home was primarily a place of shelter and survival. The cave dwellers of prehistoric times sought refuge in natural formations, using them not only to protect themselves from the elements and predators but also as places where they could come together as a community. In this context, home was synonymous with safety and survival. It was the physical space where humans could thrive and find respite from the dangers of the outside world.

As societies evolved, so too did the concept of home. In ancient Mesopotamia, Egypt, Greece, and Rome, a home was not merely a place of shelter but also a symbol of status and identity. The architecture of these homes reflected societal structures, with grandiose buildings for the wealthy and modest dwellings for the common folk. In these early civilizations, the home became a microcosm of the larger society, a place where social roles and hierarchies were reinforced. Homes were often constructed with a communal living space at the center, emphasizing family and community bonds.

During the medieval era, particularly in Europe, homes evolved into fortresses. Castles and manor houses were built not just for comfort but also for defense, with walls, moats, and drawbridges to protect inhabitants from invaders. Here, the home was both a sanctuary and a fortress—a place where one could feel safe from the chaos outside. However, it was also a place where the roles of each family member were clearly defined, with strict hierarchies and duties. The idea of home as a sanctuary persisted, but it was also a place of control and order.

With the onset of the Industrial Revolution, the concept of home underwent a significant transformation. Urbanization led to the rise of tenements and row houses, where home life was closely linked to work and economic survival. The boundaries between home and work began to blur as people moved into cities in search of employment. For many, home was no longer a refuge but a place of necessity, often cramped and overcrowded, lacking the comforts of the countryside. This period saw the rise of the nuclear family, with the home becoming a private space, distinct from the public life of work and society.

In the modern era, the idea of home has continued to evolve, influenced by technological advances, global mobility, and changing societal norms. For many, home is no longer tied to a fixed location. The rise of digital nomadism, remote work, and global migration has redefined what it means to have a home. Today, home can be a city across the world, a community of like-minded individuals, or even a digital space where one feels connected and accepted. The modern concept of home is fluid, dynamic, and deeply personal, shaped by individual experiences and identities.

Home in Language and Culture: A Deep-Seated Symbol

The enduring importance of home is evident not only in how we construct our physical dwellings but also in the language we use. The term "home" appears in countless expressions, idioms, and cultural references, reflecting its deep-seated significance in our psyche.

Consider the phrase "home run" in baseball. It signifies a triumphant return to a starting point, a safe haven where the player is beyond the reach of opponents. This term encapsulates a journey that starts and ends at home—a place of safety, celebration, and success. Similarly, the idea of a "homecoming" is a powerful metaphor in many cultures, representing a return to one's roots, to the familiar and the cherished, to a place where one is always welcomed with open arms.

We speak of "feeling at home" when we find ourselves in situations or environments where we feel comfortable, relaxed, and authentic. Conversely, we talk about feeling "homesick" when we are away from what is familiar and comforting, highlighting the emotional connection we have to the idea of home. These expressions reveal how deeply ingrained the concept of home is in our collective consciousness—a symbol of safety, belonging, and authenticity that we are always seeking to return to.

Personal Reflection: The Language of Home in My Life

For much of my life, I felt like I was living in a constant state of homesickness, even when I was physically at home. I longed for a place where I could feel truly safe and accepted, where I could take off all my masks and just be myself. But no matter where I went or what I did, that sense of home seemed to elude me. It wasn't until I began to explore the deeper meaning of home that I realized the home I was seeking was not a physical place but a feeling—a sense of peace and belonging that could only be found within myself.

Home in Religion: A Sacred Space of Divine Connection

Throughout history, the concept of home has also been deeply intertwined with spirituality and religion. Many religions view home as not just a physical space but a sacred one—a place where the divine and the earthly meet. In many spiritual traditions, the home is considered a temple, a space where one can connect with the divine and seek solace.

Christianity: In Christianity, the idea of home extends beyond the physical. It is often associated with a spiritual sanctuary, a place where one is close to God. The biblical phrase "my Father's house" is often interpreted as a reference to Heaven, the ultimate home where believers will find eternal peace and rest. Christians are taught that the body itself is a temple of the Holy Spirit, making the idea of home not just external but internal, a spiritual state of being.

Islam: In Islam, the home is considered a place of worship and spiritual growth. It is where daily prayers (Salat) are performed and where one lives according to Islamic principles. The Prophet Muhammad emphasized the importance of creating a harmonious and loving home environment, reflecting values of faith, respect, and compassion. For Muslims, home is not just a physical dwelling but a spiritual sanctuary that reflects their commitment to God.

Judaism: In Judaism, the concept of the "Promised Land" serves as a powerful metaphor for home. Historically, Jewish people have faced exile and displacement, making the idea of a spiritual home—a place where they can freely practice their faith and traditions—deeply significant. The home is often viewed as a "mikdash me'at," a small sanctuary reflecting the values of study, prayer, and family connection.

Hinduism and Buddhism: In Eastern religions like Hinduism and Buddhism, the home is seen as a sacred space for personal rituals, meditation, and spiritual growth. In Hinduism, the home is where daily worship, or "puja," is performed. In Buddhism, the concept of "going home" often transcends the physical, representing the inner sanctuary where one seeks enlightenment and liberation from suffering.

Indigenous Beliefs: For many Indigenous cultures, the concept of home is deeply connected to the land. The earth is viewed as a living, breathing entity that provides sustenance and shelter.

Home is not confined to a building or a specific place but is an expansive concept that includes the natural environment, ancestors, and spiritual beings. In these traditions, home is a communal, spiritual space that fosters a deep connection to the earth and all living beings.

How Did We Lose Our Way Home?

Despite this deep-seated yearning for home, many of us have lost our way. We live in a world that constantly pulls us in different directions, bombarding us with messages about who we should be, what we should do, and how we should live. We are conditioned from a young age to believe that success, happiness, and fulfillment lie outside of us—in material possessions, social status, and external validation. We are taught to wear masks to fit in, to conform, and to achieve, often at the cost of losing touch with our true selves.

This disconnection from our inner home often begins in childhood. As children, we are naturally attuned to our inner world. We know what we feel, what we like, and what makes us happy. But as we grow older, we learn to suppress our true feelings and desires to fit into the expectations of others. We learn to wear masks to gain approval, avoid conflict, and protect ourselves from judgment and rejection. Over time, these masks become so ingrained that we forget who we really are. We lose touch with our inner home—the place within us where we feel safe, loved and accepted for who we are.

For me, this disconnection from my inner home was compounded by the abuse and neglect I experienced in my childhood home. I learned early on to believe that I was not worthy of love, that I was somehow flawed and inadequate. These beliefs became deeply ingrained in my psyche, shaping my behavior and self-perception throughout my life. I spent years searching for a sense of home outside of myself, believing that if I could just find the right relationship, the right job, or the right place to live, I would finally feel at peace.

But no matter where I went or what I did, that sense of home seemed to elude me. It wasn't until I began to explore the deeper meaning of home and confront the wounds of my past that I realized the home I was seeking was not something I could find outside of myself. It was something I had to cultivate within—a sense of inner peace, self-acceptance, and belonging that was not dependent on external circumstances.

Home in Contemporary Spirituality: Finding the Sacred Within

In contemporary spirituality and New Age philosophies, the concept of home has shifted from being an external place to an internal state. Many modern spiritual practices emphasize the idea of finding a "home" within oneself—a place of inner peace, stability, and love that is not dependent on external circumstances. This internal home is a sanctuary of the soul, where one can retreat to find solace, strength, and clarity.

Mindfulness, meditation, and self-reflection are tools used to cultivate this inner home. These practices encourage individuals to turn inward, listen to their inner voice, and connect with their true selves. In this context, finding home is a journey of self-discovery and self-acceptance, a process of healing old wounds, releasing limiting beliefs, and embracing one's authentic self.

Personal Reflection: My Journey to Finding Home Within

For much of my life, I believed that home was something I had to find outside of myself—a place, a person, or a set of circumstances that would make me feel whole and complete. However, as I began to explore mindfulness and spiritual practices, I realized that the home I was seeking was not outside of me but within me. I began to see that true home is a state of being—a place of inner peace, self-acceptance, and love that is always available to us, no matter where we are or what we are going through.

Through meditation, journaling, and self-reflection, I began to reconnect with my inner self and heal the wounds of my past. I learned to cultivate a sense of inner peace and self-compassion, to let go of the need for external validation, and to embrace my true self with love and acceptance.

This journey has not always been easy, but it has been the most rewarding journey of my life. It has led me back to a sense of home within myself—a place where I feel safe, loved, and accepted just as I am.

Reconnecting with Our Inner Home: The Journey Begins

The good news is that no matter how far we may feel from our inner home, the path back is always available to us. It begins with a willingness to look inward, peel back the layers of conditioning, and rediscover our true selves. The journey home is a journey of healing old wounds, observing our inner world with awareness, practicing mindfulness, and embracing all parts of ourselves—our strengths and our vulnerabilities, our light and our shadows.

Through the chapters of this book, we will explore the HOME method as a pathway to finding this inner sanctuary. We will learn how to heal past wounds, observe our inner world with awareness, practice mindfulness to stay present and embrace our true selves with love and acceptance. By doing so, we can begin to create a home within ourselves—a place of deep peace, joy, and connection that is always there, no matter where we are or what we are going through.

Conclusion: The Call to Come Home

Home is not just a place; it is a state of being. It is where we are most ourselves, where we feel most connected, and where we find true peace and belonging. In a world that often pulls us in many directions, the journey home is the most important journey we can take. It is a journey back to our own hearts, our own truth, and our own source. Let us begin this journey together, and may we all find our way back to the home that has always been waiting for us—within.

Reflection Exercise: Rediscovering Your Concept of Home

To help you begin this journey, take some time to reflect on the following questions:

1. What does the word "home" mean to you?

2. When you think of home, what feelings, memories, or images come to mind?

3. Do you feel at home in your current physical space? Why or why not?

4. Have you ever felt truly at home within yourself? If so, when and where? If not, what do you think might be preventing you from feeling at home within yourself?

5. What steps can you take to begin reconnecting with your inner home?

Write down your thoughts and reflections in a journal. Remember, there are no right or wrong answers. This is your personal journey, and these reflections are meant to help you start exploring your own concept of home and what it means to you.

Chapter 2

Finding Your Tribe—The Art of Belonging and Connection Introduction: The Deep-Rooted Desire to Belong

Belonging is something we all seek. From the moment we are born, we look to connect and find our place in the world. It's natural to crave a sense of belonging, whether within our family, community, or social circles. But what happens when that sense of belonging is elusive? When the very places that are supposed to provide comfort and acceptance feel like battlegrounds or sources of rejection?

For me, the journey toward finding my tribe—my true sense of belonging—has been anything but smooth. Growing up in an abusive and neglectful environment, I learned early on that I didn't really belong in the place that was supposed to be my first home. I felt like an outsider, even within my own family. And yet, despite these challenges, I never stopped searching for that elusive feeling of connection.

I'm still on this journey today. I've made significant progress, but I would be lying if I said I've got it all figured out. There are still moments when I feel like I don't quite fit anywhere, and I notice myself falling back into old patterns of people-pleasing or withdrawing to protect myself from the fear of rejection. The difference now is that I can observe these tendencies. I don't act on them as much, and when I do, I can see them for what they are—old wounds and fears rising to the surface. It's a work in progress, and I'm learning to be patient with myself as I continue this path of healing and self-discovery.

In this chapter, I want to explore what belonging truly means and how our early experiences shape our understanding of connection. I'll share parts of my own story and reflect on how my sense of belonging (or lack thereof) has evolved over the years. Together, we'll look at why belonging is so important, how it impacts our self-worth, and what it takes to find your tribe—whether that's within your family, among friends, or, most importantly, within yourself.

The Longing for Belonging

Belonging isn't just a nice-to-have; it's a fundamental human need. It's why we naturally seek out friendships, community, and connection. We want to know that we matter to others, that we have a place in the world, and that we are valued just as we are. But what happens when, instead of feeling accepted, we are met with criticism, rejection, or even abandonment?

For me, my earliest memories of home didn't include warmth or unconditional love. Instead, I grew up in an environment where love felt conditional—based on performance, behavior, or just the whims of my parents' moods. I internalized the message that I wasn't worthy of love simply because of who I was. This belief stuck with me for a long time, shaping the way I approached relationships, friendships, and my sense of belonging.

For years, I tried to fit in wherever I could. I became a chameleon, adapting to the expectations of others in an attempt to secure their approval. But the problem with this approach was that, even when I was accepted, I never felt truly seen or understood. I wasn't showing up as my authentic self because I didn't believe my authentic self was worthy of belonging. As a result, I often felt lonely, even in the company of others.

Story: My Experience with Rejection in High School

This pattern of rejection and not fitting in followed me well into my teenage years, and one experience stands out in particular. I was in high school, assigned to a new classroom with a new group of students. These kids had been together since kindergarten—practically since birth—and were incredibly close-knit. I remember coming to school on the first day with excitement and hope, ready to make new friends and feel a part of this new group.

But that hope was quickly crushed. As I arrived, some of the students physically blocked the entrance to the classroom and told me that I didn't belong there. They made it clear that I wasn't welcome, and I stood there, frozen in disbelief. I can still feel the sting of those words even as I write this today, 29 years later. It wasn't just the insult or the humiliation; it was something much deeper. The rejection struck a chord that touched on years of feeling like I wasn't good enough like there was something fundamentally wrong with me that made people unable to accept me.

The pain was so raw and so immediate that it left a deep wound. I felt crushed to the core. The shame, the overwhelming feeling of not belonging, and the sense that I was defective in some way all rushed back to the surface. It was a feeling I was familiar with—one that had been there since childhood, but this moment brought it roaring back with such intensity that I carried it with me for years.

As a result of the incident, I was sent to the school counselor, who eventually spoke with the other students. I was allowed back into the classroom, but their dismay was obvious. They didn't talk to me for weeks, and when they finally did, I found myself gravitating toward the few outcasts of the group, the ones who had also been pushed to the fringes. Looking back now, it's clear how something like that, a single event, can stay with you for decades. It can shape how you see yourself, how you interact with others, and how you navigate the world.

For nearly 30 years, that experience influenced the way I viewed myself and my relationships. The feeling of rejection was so intense that I carried it with me as a constant reminder that I didn't belong, that there was something wrong with me, and that I had to be different, better, or more likable to be accepted. Even today, though I've done a lot of healing, I can still feel the echo of that pain. It shaped who I (thought) I was for a long time, and learning to undo that narrative has been a central part of my journey.

The Cost of Adapting to Fit In

As I moved through childhood, adolescence, and into adulthood, I continued to adapt to fit in wherever I could. I became skilled at reading people, figuring out what they wanted from me, and molding myself to meet those expectations. In some ways, this ability to adapt helped me survive emotionally. It allowed me to navigate social situations without feeling completely lost or rejected.

But there was a cost. The more I adapted to fit in, the more I lost touch with who I really was. I became so focused on being what others wanted me to be that I forgot to ask myself what I wanted or who I truly was. This disconnect between my true self and the version of myself that I presented to the world created a deep sense of loneliness, even when I was surrounded by people.

It wasn't until I began to delve deeper into my healing journey that I realized this pattern. I had been seeking external validation and connection to fill the void left by my childhood experiences. The sense of belonging I craved wasn't going to come from outside sources; it had to come from within.

Belonging Within Yourself

The most important lesson I've learned on this journey is that true belonging starts with yourself. You can't fully belong anywhere else if you don't feel at home within your own skin. This was a hard truth for me to swallow because, for most of my life, I didn't feel at home within myself. I carried a lot of shame and self-criticism rooted in the belief that I was fundamentally flawed.

Over the years, I've come to see that belonging isn't something that others give to you. It's something you create for yourself. It starts with accepting all parts of yourself—the good, the bad, and the messy. It's about learning to sit with your discomfort, your insecurities, and your fears and showing up for yourself with love and compassion.

I'm still working on this. There are days when I feel completely disconnected from myself, days when the old patterns of self-doubt and shame resurface. But now, I can observe these moments without getting lost in them. I can recognize that these are old wounds that need my attention and care, not something I need to fix or run away from.

The truth is, finding your tribe starts with finding yourself. The more you connect with your true self, the more you'll attract people who resonate with that authenticity. And when you find people who see and accept you for who you are, that's when you'll experience the true sense of belonging you've been searching for.

The Journey to Finding My Tribe

As I've healed and grown, I've started to attract more authentic relationships. I've found people who truly see me and who don't expect me to be anyone other than myself. These relationships feel different—deeper, more genuine. But even with these connections, I still struggle sometimes.

There are moments when I feel like I'm on the outside looking in, wondering if I'll ever fully belong anywhere.

And that's okay. I've come to realize that belonging is not a destination; it's a process. It's something we work on throughout our lives, and it's okay if we don't have it all figured out. What matters is that we keep showing up—for ourselves and for the people who matter to us.

I'm still learning how to belong, both to myself and to others. Some days, I feel deeply connected to my very small tribe, while other days, I feel a bit lost and disconnected. But now, I can observe these feelings without judgment. I know that they are part of the journey, and I'm learning to trust that I will find my way back to belonging—both within myself and in the world around me.

Conclusion: The Ongoing Journey of Belonging

The search for belonging is a lifelong journey. It's not about fitting in or conforming to the expectations of others. It's about finding people who see and accept you for who you are—and, most importantly, about learning to accept yourself.

I'm still on this journey, and I'm far from having all the answers. But I've learned that belonging isn't something that happens overnight. It takes time, patience, and a willingness to be vulnerable. It takes showing up as your authentic self, even when it feels scary or uncomfortable. And it takes a deep commitment to love and accept yourself, no matter what.

As you continue your own journey of belonging, I encourage you to start with yourself. Look within and ask yourself: Where do I feel at home within myself? Where do I still feel disconnected or out of place? And how can I begin to create a deeper sense of belonging, both within and with others?

Remember, this is a journey, not a race. Take your time, be patient with yourself, and trust that you will find your tribe—both within yourself and in the world around you.

Final Reflection Exercise: Exploring Your Sense of Belonging

To help you explore your sense of belonging, take some time to reflect on the following questions:

1. Do you feel a sense of belonging in your life? If so, where do you feel most at home? If not, what might be preventing you from feeling that connection?

2. In what ways have you adapted or changed yourself to fit in with others? How has this affected your sense of belonging?

3. What steps can you take to begin creating a deeper sense of belonging within yourself? How can you show up more authentically in your relationships?

4. How can you cultivate relationships with people who accept you for who you are?

Write down your thoughts and reflections in a journal. Remember, there are no right or wrong answers. This is your personal journey, and these reflections are meant to help you start exploring your own sense of belonging and how it relates to your concept of home.

Affirmations for Healing Rejection and Finding Belonging

1. I am worthy of love and acceptance, just as I am.

2. I release the belief that I am not enough.

3. I belong wherever I choose to be.

4. My value is not defined by others' opinions or actions.

5. I embrace my true self and trust that those who see me will love me for who I am.

6. The past does not define my worth.

7. I let go of the pain of rejection and make space for love and connection.

8. I am learning to feel at home within myself.

9. It's safe for me to show up as my authentic self.

10. I choose to surround myself with people who accept me for who I am.

11. I forgive myself for believing I had to change to be loved.

12. I attract people who see and appreciate my unique qualities.

13. Every day, I grow more confident in my ability to belong, just as I am.

14. I am deserving of friendships and relationships that are nurturing and supportive.

15. I honor my feelings of hurt and rejection, but I do not let them define me.

16. I trust that I will find my tribe—the people who love and accept me unconditionally.

17. I let go of the need to please others to feel worthy.

18. I allow myself to be vulnerable and open to connection.

19. I am enough, and I am loved just as I am.

20. I release the fear of rejection and welcome love and acceptance into my life.

Chapter 3

Belief Systems—The Invisible Scripts That Shape Our Lives

Introduction: The Origins of Belief Systems

"Belief systems are the blueprints for thoughts and behaviors that create your reality experience."

- Bashar

From the moment we are born, we begin to absorb beliefs about ourselves and the world around us. As children, we look to our caregivers, our families, and our communities to understand who we are and what we're worth. These early experiences, whether positive or negative, form the foundation of our belief systems—an invisible set of rules and ideas that guide our thoughts, actions, and decisions.

For many years, the belief system I developed was built on shaky ground—crafted from mixed messages, emotional neglect, and confusion. In particular, my relationship with my mother played a huge role in shaping my self-worth, body image, and my belief that I wasn't enough.

The subtle and not-so-subtle messages I received as a child stayed with me for years, influencing the way I saw myself and the world.

In this chapter, I'll share how these early experiences shaped my belief system, how they influenced my sense of self-worth and body image, and how, over time, I've worked to challenge and rewrite these harmful beliefs. I'll also explore the powerful cultural forces, like the multibillion-dollar diet industry, that continue to shape our beliefs, often without us even realizing it.

The Early Roots of My Belief System: Feeling Unimportant and Ignored

One of the most powerful influences on a child's developing belief system is the attention and emotional care they receive from their parents. For me, my mother was physically present but emotionally absent. She was often locked away in her bedroom with her coffee and book, leaving me feeling unimportant and invisible. This emotional neglect made me internalize the idea that I wasn't worth her time or attention—that my needs weren't important enough to be acknowledged.

Her apathy left a deep imprint on me, and I carried the belief that I wasn't valuable into adulthood. This belief manifested in many ways, from how I approached relationships to the way I allowed myself to be treated by others. I spent years trying to prove my worth to people, but deep down, I believed that no matter what I did, it wasn't enough.

Personal Reflection: Living with the Belief That I'm Unimportant

As a child, I couldn't understand why my mother seemed so disconnected from me. I tried in various ways to gain her attention, but her world revolved around herself, her books, and often, her obsessions with other things—particularly her weight. I internalized the belief that I didn't matter, and as an adult, I often felt invisible in relationships. I stayed quiet in meetings, avoided confrontation, and played small because I didn't believe my opinions or needs were valuable enough to be heard. Even in friendships and romantic relationships, I found myself constantly putting others' needs ahead of my own, reinforcing the belief that I wasn't important enough to deserve attention or care.

The Body Image Battle: Dieting, Obsession, and Self-Worth

One of the most insidious ways my belief system was shaped was through my mother's obsession with her weight and dieting. My mother was constantly on a diet. Even though I was a naturally skinny girl, I couldn't escape the environment of calorie counting and body scrutiny that she lived in. My mother would openly discuss her weight and calorie intake, and soon enough, she started doing the same with me.

I vividly remember how she would count calories in front of me, and sometimes for me. Even as a child, I was already being conditioned to associate my value with my body size. While I wasn't overweight, the constant talk of food and dieting made me hyperaware of my body in a way that was unnatural for a young girl. I began to develop a belief that my worth was tied to my appearance and, more specifically, to how thin I was. The result? A distorted body image and years of battling feelings of inadequacy and shame around my body.

Personal Reflection: Living with the Belief That My Body Isn't Good Enough

Even though I was skinny as a child, I remember feeling that my body was never quite right. My mother's focus on dieting made me constantly question whether I was eating too much or too little. Over time, this led to a complicated relationship between food and my body. I would obsess over how much I weighed, and if I gained even a few pounds, it felt like a personal failure.

It wasn't just my mother's dieting habits that impacted me. I grew up in a culture that reinforced the idea that to be beautiful and worthy, you had to be thin. Mannequins in stores were always tall and slender, and clothes were designed for the same ideal body type. I remember going clothes shopping and seeing how perfectly the clothes fit the mannequin, only to try them on myself and feel terrible about my own body. I internalized the belief that something was wrong with me—that I wasn't good enough unless I could look like the girls in magazines or the models in storefronts. This belief followed me for years, damaging my self-esteem and leaving me constantly striving for an impossible ideal.

The Diet Industry: A Belief System That Sells Insecurity

The diet industry is a multibillion-dollar business, and it thrives on one simple principle: insecurity. It's an industry that is built on making people feel like their bodies are never enough. Every product, every commercial, every new fad diet is designed to convince us that we need to change ourselves in order to be worthy—worthy of love, worthy of attention, and worthy of happiness.

This toxic belief system starts young, especially for girls. From a young age, we are bombarded with images of what an "ideal" body looks like, whether it's in movies, on TV, or in advertisements. We're told that to be beautiful means to be thin and that thinness is a prerequisite for success and happiness. Over time, these messages become part of our belief system, shaping the way we see ourselves and the world.

For me, these cultural messages worked hand in hand with the beliefs I had developed at home.

My mother's obsession with her weight was simply a reflection of the larger culture we lived in—one that placed immense value on appearance and thinness. The diet industry may have profited from these beliefs, but for people like me, they resulted in years of self-loathing, body image issues, and a complicated relationship with food.

Personal Reflection: Breaking Free from the Diet Culture

It took me a long time to realize just how deeply these beliefs about my body and weight had shaped me. Even when I wasn't actively dieting, I still carried the underlying assumption that my body wasn't good enough. I would criticize myself in the mirror, feeling like I didn't measure up to the impossible standards I had been conditioned to believe were normal.

As I started to do the work of healing my belief system, I began to see how harmful these beliefs were. I started to question the messages I had absorbed from my mother, from society, and from the diet industry. I realized that my worth had nothing to do with my weight or appearance. This shift in my beliefs didn't happen overnight, but it was a crucial part of reclaiming my self-worth.

The Mixed Messages: You're Stupid… But So Smart

If my mother's emotional neglect and obsession with her weight taught me that I wasn't valuable, the mixed messages I received about my intelligence created a deep sense of confusion and self-doubt. My parents would often call me stupid to my face, especially when I made mistakes or failed to meet their expectations. But then, in front of their friends, they would boast about how smart I was, painting a picture of me that I didn't recognize.

This contradiction left me feeling lost. Was I smart or stupid? Was I capable or incapable? The confusion created a belief that I was somehow both—that I could be smart in front of others, but deep down, I was actually inadequate. This belief followed me for years, manifesting as self-doubt in almost every area of my life. Even when I achieved something, I felt like I didn't deserve it, like I had somehow tricked people into thinking I was smarter than I really was.

Personal Reflection: Carrying the Belief That I'm Stupid

For most of my life, I carried the belief that I wasn't smart enough, even when there was evidence to the contrary. I struggled with imposter syndrome, feeling like I had to overcompensate just to keep up with the expectations placed on me. Whether it was in school, work, or social situations, I often felt like I was pretending—wearing a mask of competence to hide the fact that I wasn't good enough. This belief created anxiety and held me back from taking risks, trying new things, or stepping into my full potential.

How Early Beliefs Shape Our Lives

Our belief systems are powerful because they operate largely in the background, influencing our thoughts, behaviors, and decisions without us being fully aware of them. The beliefs I developed in childhood—beliefs that I wasn't important, that my body wasn't good enough, and that I wasn't smart—became the lens through which I viewed the world. They shaped how I saw myself, how I interacted with others, and what I believed I deserved.

The most damaging part of these belief systems is that they often go unchallenged for years. I carried these beliefs with me well into adulthood, rarely questioning whether they were true. Instead, I found evidence to support them. Every time I felt ignored, I reinforced the belief that I was unimportant. Every time I looked in the mirror and didn't see perfection, I confirmed the belief that my body wasn't good enough. These beliefs became self-fulfilling prophecies, shaping the choices I made and the paths I took.

Challenging and Rewriting Limiting Beliefs

It wasn't until I started to do the inner work of healing that I began to challenge these beliefs.

One of the first steps in this process was recognizing that these beliefs weren't truths about who I was—they were stories I had learned to tell myself based on my childhood experiences. They

were the result of my parents' words and actions, as well as the cultural messages I had absorbed, not an accurate reflection of my worth.

I had to learn to become aware of these invisible scripts running in the background. It wasn't easy. For so many years, I had simply accepted these beliefs as facts, and it took a lot of self-reflection and therapy to start questioning them. But once I did, I began to see how these beliefs were holding me back and keeping me from living a fuller, more authentic life.

Personal Reflection: The Moment I Realized My Beliefs Weren't True

There wasn't a single "aha" moment when I realized that my beliefs about myself weren't true. It was more of a slow unraveling, a series of small moments where I began to see the cracks in the stories I had been telling myself. One of the most powerful moments came when I was in therapy, talking about how I always felt unimportant in my relationships. My therapist gently asked me, "What if the problem isn't that you're unimportant but that you've been conditioned to believe that you are?"

That simple question shifted something in me. It made me realize that my belief wasn't a fact—it was a story I had learned based on how my mother treated me. From there, I began to challenge the belief more actively, looking for evidence in my life that proved I wasn't unimportant. I started noticing the ways in which people valued me, how my friends and loved ones showed up for me, and how my contributions mattered.

The Long Process of Rewiring Beliefs

Rewriting the belief systems that have shaped your life isn't something that happens overnight. It's a long, often painful process of unlearning the stories you've told yourself and replacing them with new, healthier beliefs. For me, this process has been ongoing, and there are still days when the old beliefs resurface.

But the difference now is that I can recognize them for what they are. When I hear the voice in my head telling me that I'm stupid, unimportant, or not good enough, I can step back and question it. Is this belief true? Or is it just an old script that no longer serves me?

The more I practice challenging these beliefs, the easier it becomes to rewrite them. I've learned to replace the old beliefs with new affirmations—statements of truth about who I really am. I am important. I am worthy. I am capable. These new beliefs have slowly begun to take root, though I know the process of reinforcing them will continue for the rest of my life.

Personal Reflection: Living with New Beliefs

Living with new beliefs about myself has been both liberating and terrifying. On the one hand, it's freeing to no longer feel trapped by the old stories of unworthiness and inadequacy. But on the other hand, stepping into a new sense of self-worth feels unfamiliar, almost like walking into uncharted territory.

There are days when I feel confident in my new beliefs when I trust in my abilities and know that I deserve to be seen and heard. But there are also days when the old beliefs come creeping back in, whispering that I'm still not good enough. On those days, I remind myself that this is a process. Healing isn't linear, and it's okay to have setbacks. The important thing is that I keep moving forward, even when it feels hard.

How to Identify and Change Your Limiting Beliefs

If you're carrying limiting beliefs from your past, you're not alone. We all have belief systems that have been shaped by our early experiences, and many of us go through life without ever questioning them. But the good news is that it's never too late to challenge and change those beliefs. Here are some steps you can take to start identifying and rewriting the beliefs that are holding you back:

1. Become Aware of Your Beliefs: The first step in changing your beliefs is becoming aware of them. Start paying attention to the thoughts and stories that run through your mind. What do you tell yourself about who you are and what you're capable of? Are these beliefs empowering or limiting?

2. Question the Beliefs: Once you've identified a limiting belief, start questioning it. Ask yourself where this belief came from. Is it something you learned in childhood? Did someone else put that belief on you? And most importantly, is the belief true? Often, our beliefs are based on past experiences, not on objective truth.

3. Look for Evidence Against the Belief: One of the most effective ways to challenge a limiting belief is to look for evidence that disproves it. If you believe you're unworthy, look for moments in your life when you were loved and valued. If you believe you're stupid, think of times when you succeeded or learned something new.

4. Create New Beliefs: Once you've challenged a limiting belief, start replacing it with a new, healthier belief. This could be an affirmation

like, "I am worthy of love" or "I am capable and intelligent." Write these new beliefs down and repeat them to yourself regularly.

5. Practice Self-Compassion: Changing your belief system takes time, and it's important to be gentle with yourself during the process. There will be setbacks, and that's okay. The important thing is that you keep moving forward and continue challenging the beliefs that no longer serve you.

Affirmations for Rewriting Your Belief System

Here are some affirmations that have helped me rewire my own beliefs. You can use these as a starting point or create your own based on the specific beliefs you're working to change.

1. I am worthy of love and attention.
2. I am intelligent and capable.
3. My value is not defined by others' opinions.
4. I am important, and my contributions matter.
5. I release the belief that I am not enough.
6. I am deserving of success and happiness.
7. I trust in my abilities and intelligence.
8. My past does not define my worth.
9. I am learning to love and accept myself fully.
10. I am capable of rewriting my own story.

Chapter 4

The Inner Child—Healing the Fragile Parts of Ourselves

Introduction: The Subtle Influence of the Inner Child

The inner child is not merely a symbolic figure from our past. It represents the part of us that holds our earliest wounds, our unmet needs, and our most fragile emotions. For much of my life, I was unaware that my inner child was deeply influencing my decisions—how I saw myself, the relationships I chose, and how I responded to conflict or vulnerability. Having grown up with neglect, emotional abuse, and even physical abuse, I developed an inner child who was scared, fragile, and desperate for love and security.

For years, my wounded inner child ran the show without me even realizing it. I chose partners and friends who mirrored the dynamics of my childhood—people who made me feel unimportant or unsafe. I was unknowingly repeating the same painful patterns, hoping to "fix" the past, but I didn't understand that healing wouldn't come from recreating those relationships. It wasn't until I began to acknowledge my inner child, observe her with compassion, and build trust with her that true healing began.

In this chapter, I want to share my personal journey of healing my inner child. The process was hard and painful at times, but learning to build trust with that scared little girl inside me was one of the most important things I've ever done. Healing my inner child wasn't just about resolving the past—it was about reclaiming my life in the present. One of the greatest rewards for facing my fears and embracing my wounded inner child has been finding myself in a healthy relationship today, where both my partner and I handle the appearance of our inner children with care and compassion.

The Inner Child in the Shadows: How Unhealed Wounds Hijack Our Lives

For many years, I didn't realize that my inner child was controlling so much of my adult life. I didn't see that my childhood wounds—emotional neglect, criticism, and even physical abuse—were still influencing my decisions, especially in relationships. I repeatedly chose partners who were emotionally unavailable, critical, or neglectful without understanding why. These partners mirrored the dynamics I had grown up with, and though painful, it was familiar. My inner child was still searching for the love, approval, and safety that had been missing from my early years.

What I've come to understand is that many of us are completely unaware of how deeply our childhood traumas affect us. Some people don't even realize they have childhood trauma because they've pushed the painful memories so deep into their subconscious that they believe they've "forgotten" them. But the truth is, we don't forget. We relive these traumas through our actions, choices, and relationships, often without realizing it.

We repeat the same destructive patterns—choosing abusive or emotionally distant partners, engaging in self-sabotaging behaviors, or staying stuck in toxic environments. These patterns are our inner child's way of trying to resolve what was never resolved in childhood. The trauma may be buried, but it continues to hijack our lives until we face it head-on.

Personal Reflection: Repeating the Painful Patterns of My Childhood

Looking back now, it's clear to me how my childhood trauma shaped my relationships. I kept choosing partners who made me feel the same way my parents had—unimportant, unsafe, and unloved. I repeated these patterns because my wounded inner child was still trying to fix the past. She was still hoping that this time, she would finally get the love and care she had always longed for.

For years, I didn't see the connection between my childhood experiences and the choices I was making in my adult life. All I knew was that I kept ending up in the same painful situations, no matter how hard I tried to avoid them. It wasn't until I started doing deep inner child work that I realized the root of the problem. My inner child wasn't broken—she was scared, fragile, and desperately seeking the love and security she had never received. But true healing couldn't come from anyone else. It had to come from me.

Building Trust with the Inner Child: A Hard and Painful Process

Healing the inner child is not a quick or easy process. In fact, it's one of the hardest and most painful things I've ever done. For so long, I had pushed my inner child's pain aside, pretending it didn't exist. When I finally started to face her, it was overwhelming. All the fear, shame, and sadness I had buried for so many years came rushing to the surface. It was incredibly difficult to sit with those emotions, to witness her pain, and to acknowledge how deeply wounded she was.

But healing the inner child requires building trust. For years, I had ignored or scolded my inner child, treating her just as harshly as my parents had treated me. She had no reason to trust me. I had to show her, over and over again, that I was there for her—that I wouldn't abandon her or dismiss her feelings anymore. This took time and patience. Slowly, as I began to approach her with compassion and understanding, she began to trust me.

Personal Reflection: The Painful Process of Earning My Inner Child's Trust

I remember the moment I realized that my inner child didn't trust me. I had spent so many years silencing her, trying to ignore her pain, that she had learned not to rely on me for comfort. When I first started doing inner child work, I would try to console her, but she didn't respond. It felt like no matter how much love I tried to offer, she wouldn't let me in.

At first, this was incredibly frustrating and heartbreaking, but I understood that she needed time.

Just like a scared child needs time to trust a new caregiver, my inner child needed to see that I was committed to her healing. Little by little, I started showing up for her—not just when it was convenient, but every day. I checked in with her, listened to her needs, and offered her comfort. Slowly, she began to trust me, and the healing process could truly begin.

Breaking the Cycle: Observing with Compassion Instead of Scolding

One of the most important lessons I've learned is that my inner child doesn't need fixing—she needs understanding. For years, I tried to scold her into being stronger, to push away the fear, sadness, and vulnerability she felt. But the real breakthrough came when I stopped trying to fix her and started to observe her with compassion.

Instead of criticizing myself for feeling scared or weak, I began to see those emotions as messages from my inner child. She wasn't acting out because she was flawed; she was acting out because she was hurting. The more I learned to observe her pain with compassion, the more I could console her, offering her the love and care she had always needed.

Personal Reflection: Consoling the Fragile Little Girl Within

There was a time in my healing process when I faced a situation that triggered all my old wounds. I felt small, scared, and deeply inadequate. In the past, I would have pushed those feelings away, ashamed of my vulnerability. But this time, I did something different. I closed my eyes and imagined myself as a little girl—fragile and scared. I asked her what she needed, and I sat with her pain, offering her comfort instead of criticism.

It wasn't easy. It felt unnatural at first, but over time, I learned to console that little girl inside of me. I reminded her that it was okay to feel scared, that she was loved, and that she was safe now. Each time I did this, I felt a little more whole, and my inner child began to heal.

Seeing the Inner Child in Others: Compassion and Detachment

One of the most powerful realizations I've had is that many adults who act out—whether in anger, cruelty, or abusive behaviors—are often acting from the wounds of their own inner child.

When we're aware enough to recognize this, it becomes easier to feel compassion, even when someone is behaving in hurtful ways.

That doesn't mean we have to tolerate abusive behavior or stay in toxic situations—boundaries are essential. But when we understand that many people are acting from their unhealed inner child, we can choose to detach with love. We can walk away from harmful situations while still holding compassion for the other person's pain. Every child, no matter what they've been through, deserves to feel safe and loved. There's no such thing as a bad child—only a wounded one.

Personal Reflection: Recognizing the Inner Child in Others

There have been times when people in my life have been deeply unkind or even cruel. In the past, I would have responded with anger or defensiveness, but as I became more aware of my own inner child, I began to see the inner child in others. I realized that their hurtful behavior often came from their own unresolved wounds.

One person in particular was incredibly hurtful toward me, and at first, I took it personally. But as I reflected on the situation, I began to see that their behavior mirrored the same dynamics I had experienced in childhood. This person's inner child was wounded, too, just like mine had been. Instead of responding with anger, I was able to detach with love. I didn't excuse their behavior, but I chose to see it through the lens of compassion. I set boundaries to protect myself while still wishing for their healing.

The Ultimate Reward: Finding Love and Healing in a Healthy Relationship

After years of repeating the same painful patterns, I am now in a healthy, loving relationship—one that is built on mutual respect, compassion, and understanding. This relationship is one of the greatest rewards of my healing journey. My inner child still makes an appearance from time to time, especially in moments of vulnerability, but now both my partner and I are aware of it. When those moments arise, we handle them with care, compassion, and patience.

My partner and I understand that the inner child is not something to be feared or scolded. We know that when my inner child or her inner child shows up, it's a sign that there's a wound that needs attention. Instead of reacting defensively or judgmentally, we create space for understanding. This is the ultimate reward for facing my fear and embracing the little wounded girl inside of me—I have learned to nurture and heal her, and as a result, I now have a relationship that nurtures and supports me as well.

Personal Reflection: Nurturing the Inner Child in My Relationship

One of the most beautiful aspects of my relationship is the way my partner and I support each other's inner child. When my inner child feels scared or triggered, my partner offers me the space to feel those emotions without judgment. She doesn't try to "fix" me; instead, she listens, holds space, and helps me process those feelings. The same goes for her. When her inner child is triggered, I offer the same compassion and understanding.

This mutual recognition of our inner children has deepened our relationship in ways I never thought possible. We both understand that while we are adults, we still carry the wounds of our past. But now, instead of letting those wounds control us, we approach them with compassion, and we heal together.

Recreating the Wounds Until We Heal: The Work of Alice Miller and John Bradshaw

One of the most profound realizations I've had during my healing journey is that we often unconsciously recreate the wounds of our childhood in our adult lives. This concept is central to the work of Alice Miller and John Bradshaw, who both explored the ways in which unhealed childhood trauma influences our adult relationships and behaviors.

Alice Miller, in her groundbreaking book The Drama of the Gifted Child, explains that many of us carry the pain of our childhood into adulthood, often without even realizing it. We repeat the same emotional dynamics, choosing relationships that mirror the unresolved pain of our early years. Until we acknowledge and heal these wounds, we are destined to replay the same patterns, hoping each time for a different outcome.

John Bradshaw, in his book Homecoming: Reclaiming and Championing Your Inner Child, builds on this idea by emphasizing the importance of nurturing and healing the inner child. He argues that until we do this work—until we face the pain of our childhood and offer our inner child the love and care they need—we will continue to act out those wounds in our adult lives.

Personal Reflection: Repeating the Wounds Until I Saw What I Needed to Heal

As I look back, I can clearly see how I unconsciously recreated the wounds of my childhood. I chose partners who were emotionally distant, just like my parents had been. I allowed myself to be treated poorly because, deep down, I believed that's what I deserved. Each relationship felt like a repeat of my childhood dynamics, and it wasn't until I began healing my inner child that I understood why.

My inner child was still searching for the love and safety she had never received. But I realized that no partner could give me what I needed. Healing had to come from within. I had to be the one to offer my inner child the love, safety, and compassion she had been searching for all along.

The Path to Healing: Observing, Consoling, and Integrating

Healing the inner child is a process that requires patience, compassion, and a willingness to face the wounds of the past. It's about learning to observe our triggers with curiosity rather than judgment and offering ourselves comfort instead of criticism. When we feel the familiar sting of rejection, inadequacy, or fear, it's often our inner child crying out for attention. In those moments, we can choose to console her rather than scold her.

As we begin to console our inner child and offer her the love and care she never received, we start to heal. Over time, the inner child becomes less of a separate, wounded part of us and more integrated into the whole of who we are. She becomes a reminder of our resilience, our capacity for healing, and our ability to love ourselves unconditionally.

Affirmations for Healing the Inner Child

Here are some affirmations that have helped me heal and nurture my inner child. You can use these as a starting point or create your own to reflect the specific wounds you are working to heal.

1. I am safe now, and I protect my inner child with love.
2. I see and honor the pain of my inner child with compassion.
3. It's okay to feel scared, and I will be here to comfort you.
4. I release the need to recreate the wounds of my childhood.
5. I am worthy of love, care, and attention.
6. I forgive myself for the times I was harsh with my inner child.
7. I am learning to console and nurture the fragile parts of myself.
8. My inner child is a part of my wholeness, and I embrace her with love.
9. I am patient with my healing journey, and I trust in the process.
10. I am not defined by the pain of my past—I am defined by the love I give to myself now.

Chapter 5

The Mirror Effect—Seeing Yourself in the Reflection of Others

Introduction: Relationships as Mirrors

Relationships offer us more than companionship, love, or even conflict—they provide one of the most powerful tools for self-awareness. Every person we connect with reflects some aspect of ourselves back to us, whether we like what we see or not. This is the essence of the mirror effect: through our interactions with others, we see parts of ourselves that might otherwise remain hidden. Sometimes, those reflections show us our strengths and growth, but more often than not, they reveal our unresolved pain, insecurities, and unhealed aspects.

For years, I struggled with difficult relationships, unaware that they were reflecting my inner state. I was drawn to people who brought up old hurts, but I didn't realize that it was their ability to trigger me that made them mirrors for my unhealed wounds. The mirror effect isn't about others showing us how they are but how we are—how we respond, react, and navigate the world. The key to personal growth lies in recognizing these reflections and using them to learn about ourselves.

In this chapter, we will explore how the mirror effect can be used as a powerful tool for self-observation. I'll share some personal insights and experiences and guide you through recognizing the mirrors in your own relationships. The goal is to help you stop seeing others as the cause of your emotional reactions and start using those reflections to understand yourself better.

What Is the Mirror Effect?

At its core, the mirror effect is the idea that people in our lives—whether they are romantic partners, friends, or even coworkers—act as mirrors, reflecting aspects of our inner world back to us. This concept can be difficult to accept because it means that our emotional reactions to others are not just about them—they are about us. When someone makes you feel frustrated, angry, or inadequate, they are often reflecting back something within you that has yet to be addressed.

It's important to note that this doesn't mean that other people are always right or that their behavior is justified. Instead, it means that our reactions to them provide clues to our own emotional landscape. The mirror effect gives us a chance to observe ourselves, not to place blame or judgment, but to understand where we are emotionally and what might need healing or attention.

The Mirror in Romantic Relationships: Learning to See Yourself

Romantic relationships often bring out the strongest reflections because they tend to be the most emotionally charged. In my own life, I've found that my partners have always been the clearest mirrors, showing me both my strengths and my vulnerabilities. In the past, when I felt ignored or undervalued in relationships, I would blame my partner for making me feel that way. It took time and a lot of self-reflection to realize that my feelings weren't just about their behavior—they were also about my own sense of worth.

For example, there was a time when I was in a relationship where I constantly felt unappreciated. I found myself resenting my partner for not showing enough affection or gratitude. But when I took a step back and used the mirror effect to observe myself, I realized that my frustration was rooted in my own insecurities about not being enough. My partner wasn't causing my insecurity—they were reflecting it back to me.

By recognizing this, I was able to shift the focus from blaming them to understanding what I needed to work on within myself. I began to ask myself why I felt unworthy of appreciation and worked on building my own self-esteem. As a result, not only did I feel more secure, but the dynamic in the relationship also improved because I was no longer looking to my partner to fill a void that only I could address.

Seeing Yourself Through Conflict: Emotions as Reflections

One of the clearest ways the mirror effect shows up is in conflict. When someone triggers a strong emotional reaction in you—whether it's anger, frustration, or hurt—it's usually a sign that they are reflecting something within you that needs attention. It's easy to get caught up in the drama of conflict and point fingers at the other person, but that approach rarely leads to personal growth.

Instead, the mirror effect invites us to observe our reactions and ask ourselves why we are so triggered. What is it about this person's behavior that is causing such a strong emotional response? Often, the answer lies within us. The emotions we feel are not just reactions to the other person's behavior; they are reflections of unresolved emotions or beliefs we hold about ourselves.

Personal Reflection: Learning from Conflict

I remember one particularly challenging friendship where every conversation seemed to lead to an argument. I often left our interactions feeling frustrated and hurt, convinced that my friend was the problem. But as I started exploring the mirror effect, I realized that my friend wasn't causing my frustration—she was reflecting my own tendency to avoid conflict. Her direct and confrontational style was something I was uncomfortable with because I had always avoided difficult conversations, fearing that they would lead to rejection.

By recognizing this reflection, I was able to approach conflict differently. I stopped blaming my friend for making me uncomfortable and instead used our interactions as an opportunity to confront my own fear of conflict. Over time, I became more comfortable with difficult conversations, and as a result, our friendship improved because I was no longer avoiding the issues that needed to be addressed.

Recognizing Patterns: The Repeated Reflections of Our Lives

One of the most revealing aspects of the mirror effect is noticing patterns in your relationships. Have you ever found yourself in different relationships but dealing with the same issues over and over again? This isn't a coincidence. It's a sign that the same unhealed parts of you are being reflected in every new situation until you acknowledge and address them.

In my case, I noticed that I kept ending up in relationships where I felt emotionally neglected. It didn't matter if the person I was with was entirely different from the last—somehow, I found myself feeling the same way. At first, I thought I just had bad luck with partners, but as I reflected more deeply, I realized that this was a pattern that had more to do with me than with them. The emotional neglect I had experienced growing up was still unresolved, and it was being reflected back to me in every relationship until I finally dealt with it.

Once I started addressing the root of the issue—my fear of abandonment and the belief that I wasn't worthy of emotional attention—I stopped attracting relationships that mirrored those dynamics. Instead, I began to experience relationships where I felt seen, valued, and respected.

Using the Mirror Effect as a Tool for Self-Observation

The beauty of the mirror effect is that it gives us the opportunity to observe ourselves without judgment. When we recognize that the people around us are reflecting our inner state, we can stop blaming them for how we feel and start using those reflections as tools for growth. This doesn't mean we excuse bad behavior or tolerate unhealthy relationships, but it does mean that we can learn from every interaction.

Here's how to use the mirror effect as a tool for self-observation:

- Pay Attention to Your Reactions: The next time someone triggers an emotional reaction in you—whether it's frustration, anger, or insecurity—pause and ask yourself what part of you is being reflected.

Is there an unresolved belief or wound that's being brought to the surface?

- Look for Patterns: Reflect on your past relationships and interactions. Do you notice any recurring themes or patterns? If so, what might those patterns be telling you about yourself and what you need to heal?

- Separate the Reflection from the Person: Remember that the person triggering you isn't the problem—they are simply holding up a mirror. Try to separate their behavior from your emotional reaction and focus on what your reaction is telling you about yourself.

- Practice Self-Compassion: The mirror effect can reveal painful truths about ourselves, but it's important to approach this process with compassion. We're all works in progress, and the goal is to learn and grow, not to judge or criticize ourselves.

Exercise: Reflecting on Your Relationships

This exercise will help you use the mirror effect to better understand your emotional responses and patterns in your relationships. It's a tool for self-observation, not self-criticism, so approach it with curiosity and openness.

1. Identify a Recent Emotional Reaction: Think about a recent interaction with someone that triggered a strong emotional response—whether it was anger, frustration, sadness, or insecurity. Write down what happened and how you felt.

2. Examine the Reflection: Ask yourself, "What is this person reflecting back to me?" Is it an insecurity, a fear, or a belief about

yourself? Try to connect the dots between their behavior and your emotional reaction.

3.	Look for Patterns: Think about whether you've had similar emotional reactions in the past with other people. Is there a pattern of being triggered in similar ways? What might this tell you about what you need to work on within yourself?

4.	Take Responsibility for Your Growth: Instead of blaming the other person for your emotional reaction, focus on what you can learn from the reflection. How can you use this experience to grow or heal?

5.	Create a New Response: Based on what you've learned, think about how you can respond differently next time. Instead of reacting out of pain or insecurity, how can you approach the situation from a place of self-awareness and growth?

Affirmations for Self-Observation and Growth

Here are some affirmations to help you navigate the mirror effect and use it as a tool for personal growth:

1.	I recognize that my relationships reflect my inner world.

2.	I observe my emotional reactions without judgment, knowing they offer insights into my healing.

3.	I take responsibility for my own growth and healing.

4.	I am open to learning from my relationships and seeing what they reveal about myself.

5.   I release the need to blame others for my emotional triggers.

6.   I approach my patterns with curiosity and compassion.

7.   I use the mirror effect as a tool for self-awareness and personal growth.

8.   I welcome the lessons my relationships teach me.

9.   I trust that every emotional reaction is an opportunity for healing.

10.   I am committed to my growth and embrace what my relationships reveal.

Chapter 6

Introducing the HOME Method—A Practical Tool for Everyday Healing

Introduction: My Journey HOME

I created the HOME Method not as a quick fix or a rigid system but as a tool, I desperately needed to help me cope with life's most difficult moments. After years of therapy, self-reflection, and inner work, I realized I needed a structured way to understand and navigate my emotions, my pain, and my personal growth. The HOME Method became my anchor, a way to return to myself when life felt overwhelming. It didn't magically make my problems disappear, but it gave me a roadmap to healing—a process I'm still in today.

I'm sharing the HOME Method with you not because it's a "cure-all" but because it has been a source of profound healing for me. It's a simple framework that I use daily to bring awareness to my emotional state and to address the pain I've carried for so long. Healing is not a destination, and neither is this method—it's a journey, one that I hope will bring you closer to yourself, just as it has for me. Each time I return "HOME," I learn something new about myself, and I'm reminded that healing is an ongoing, evolving process.

The HOME Method: Healing, Observing, Mindfulness, Embracing

The HOME Method stands for Healing, Observing, Mindfulness, and Embracing. These four steps guide you through the process of self-awareness, allowing you to create space for your emotions, reflect on what they're trying to tell you and respond to life with more clarity and compassion. For me, the HOME Method has been a lifeline, especially during times when I felt lost or overwhelmed by my emotions.

It's important to note that healing through this method doesn't mean the pain completely disappears. I still have difficult moments, but now, when I'm triggered, I have a practice that helps me cope. I can pause, return to these four steps, and feel my way through the moment rather than react impulsively or drown in old wounds.

Step 1: Healing—Recognizing That Everything Is Part of Your Healing Process

The first step in the HOME Method is Healing. It begins with recognizing that every situation, especially the painful ones, offers an opportunity for healing. When life throws challenges your way—whether it's a difficult conversation, an unexpected loss, or a trigger from the past—those experiences are not random. They are part of your healing journey, helping you uncover wounds that still need attention.

Healing is not linear, and it's not something we ever "complete." For me, acknowledging that I'm always in the process of healing has been both humbling and empowering. I used to think that one day, I'd wake up fully healed, with no pain left to process. But life doesn't work that way. Healing is cyclical, and new layers of old wounds often emerge as we grow. What has shifted for me through the HOME Method is my ability to see these moments as opportunities for growth rather than setbacks.

Example: There was a time when I felt completely defeated by life's circumstances. The weight of my past trauma and the pain of losing my sister felt unbearable. I had no choice but to look for healing in every situation that brought up those emotions. Instead of avoiding or suppressing the pain, I began to see it as part of my journey. Each time I was triggered, it wasn't just an old wound reopening—it was a chance for me to heal another layer. This mindset shift has allowed me to approach difficult moments with more compassion for myself and the process of healing.

Step 2: Observing—Becoming a Witness to Your Emotions

The second step is Observing. Once you've recognized that a situation is part of your healing, the next step is to observe it. Observation is about stepping back from the emotional storm and simply noticing what's happening within you. This can be incredibly powerful because it creates space between you and your emotions.

Before I developed this step, I often felt overwhelmed by my feelings. I would become so caught up in the pain, the anger, or the sadness that I couldn't see beyond it. But when I started practicing observation, I learned to witness my emotions without judgment. I could feel sadness without becoming sad. I could observe anger without reacting to it. This is not always easy, and there are still moments when I slip back into old patterns, but the HOME Method has given me a tool to navigate those moments with more awareness.

Example: When I feel triggered, like during an argument with someone close to me, I now try to observe my emotions rather than react immediately. I notice where the anger or sadness is coming from, and more often than not, it's tied to old wounds or unresolved issues. By simply observing without judgment, I give myself space to process the emotion before it escalates into something more damaging.

Step 3: Mindfulness—Responding with Presence and Calm

The third step in the HOME Method is Mindfulness. After observing your emotions, the next step is to mindfully respond to the situation. Mindfulness means staying grounded in the present moment and making conscious choices about how you want to respond rather than reacting out of habit or pain.

For me, mindfulness has been a game-changer. There were times in my life when I acted impulsively out of hurt, anger, or fear, only to regret my actions later. Mindfulness helps me pause and consider what's happening inside of me before I respond to the world outside of me. It's not about being perfect or always responding with calm—trust me, there are still moments when I lose my cool—but it's about making more intentional choices.

Example: In the past, when someone criticized me, I would immediately go into defense mode, reacting out of fear that I wasn't good enough. Through mindfulness, I've learned to pause and take a breath. Instead of reacting out of old wounds, I can now respond more calmly and thoughtfully. Sometimes, that means speaking my truth; other times, it means walking away and revisiting the conversation later when I've had time to process it.

Step 4: Embracing—Welcoming the Lessons of the Experience

The final step is Embracing. After you've moved through the process of healing, observing, and responding mindfully, it's time to embrace the lesson that the situation has offered you.

Embracing is about accepting what the moment has taught you and using it as a stepping stone on your path to growth.

One of the most transformative things I've learned through the HOME Method is that every situation, no matter how painful, has something to teach us. It doesn't mean that we have to like the pain or wish for difficult experiences, but embracing them allows us to integrate the lessons they bring. This process has helped me soften my resistance to life's challenges and trust that every experience is part of my journey.

Example: After any particularly challenging situation—whether it's a difficult conversation, a triggering event, or a moment of self-doubt—I take time to reflect on the lesson. Sometimes, it's immediate, but often, it takes days or weeks for the clarity to come. I've learned to embrace the process of growth, even when it's uncomfortable, and to see the challenges as opportunities to deepen my connection with myself.

The HOME Method in Action

Here's how you can use the HOME Method in your daily life:

1.   **Healing:** When you find yourself in a difficult situation or emotional state, remind yourself that this moment is happening for

your healing. What part of you is being called to heal? What old wounds are surfacing?

2. **Observing:** Take a step back and observe your emotions without judgment. What are you feeling? Where do you feel it in your body? Notice your thoughts and reactions without getting caught up in them.

3. **Mindfulness:** After observing your emotions, mindfully choose how you want to respond. What is the most compassionate, thoughtful way to address this situation? Can you stay grounded in the present moment and avoid reacting out of old patterns?

4. **Embracing:** Once the moment has passed, reflect on the lesson. What did this experience teach you about yourself? How can you use this insight to grow? Embrace the process of healing, knowing that it's a lifelong journey.

Affirmations for Using the HOME Method

Here are some affirmations to help you incorporate the HOME Method into your daily life:

1. I acknowledge that every challenge is an opportunity for my healing.
2. I observe my emotions with compassion and curiosity.
3. I respond to difficult situations mindfully and calmly.
4. I embrace the lessons from each experience with openness and gratitude.
5. I trust myself to navigate life's challenges with grace and awareness.
6. Healing is a process, and I am patient with myself as I grow.

Chapter 7

Inner Dialogue—Navigating Triggers with Self-Awareness Through the HOME Method

Introduction: The Role of Inner Dialogue in Emotional Growth

In moments of emotional tension, we often feel the urge to react—whether it's through anger, shutting down, or withdrawing. But when we learn to engage in inner dialogue, we create space to understand what's happening beneath the surface. This practice helps us process our emotions, regulate our responses, and make sense of the complex feelings that often arise in triggering situations.

Inner dialogue is not about silencing or controlling our emotions but about listening to them with curiosity and compassion. It's about slowing down enough to ask ourselves, "What is really happening here?" When paired with the HOME Method—Healing, Observing, Mindfulness, and Embracing—inner dialogue becomes an essential tool for navigating difficult moments with kindness and clarity.

The true power of the HOME Method lies in how it guides us back to ourselves in moments of emotional upheaval. When you pause, engage in inner dialogue, and apply the four steps of HOME, you learn how to turn even the most triggering situations into opportunities for healing and growth.

Why Inner Dialogue Is Key to Growth

Inner dialogue is an ongoing conversation with yourself. It helps you recognize your emotions in

real-time and see them for what they are—a reflection of your inner world. Most of our strongest emotional reactions are not about the present moment but are connected to deeper fears, unresolved emotions, or past experiences. By engaging in compassionate inner dialogue, we can unpack these layers and get to the root of what's really happening.

For example, you might find yourself snapping at someone over something small. Upon reflection, it might become clear that your reaction wasn't about the current situation but about feeling ignored or unimportant, which ties back to childhood experiences. The beauty of inner dialogue is that it gives you the tools to address these underlying emotions without getting lost in them.

Using the HOME Method to Manage Triggers with Inner Dialogue

When you encounter a trigger, here's how to use the HOME Method as part of your inner dialogue practice:

1. **Healing:** Acknowledge that the situation is happening for your healing. Triggers are not random; they are opportunities for growth. Remind yourself that this moment is showing you an unresolved wound that needs your attention.

   Questions to ask yourself:
   - What is this situation bringing up for me emotionally?

- How might this experience be part of my healing journey?

- What old wound or unresolved feeling is this moment tapping into?

2. **Observing:** Step back and observe your emotions and reactions without judgment. Ask yourself: What part of me is reacting? Is this about the current situation, or is it tied to something deeper?

Questions to ask yourself:

- What am I feeling right now—physically and emotionally?

- What triggered this reaction? Is it really about this moment?

- Where have I felt this way before? Is this a familiar feeling from my past?

3. **Mindfulness:** Respond mindfully to the situation. Take a deep breath, ground yourself in the present moment, and choose how you want to address the trigger. Focus on staying calm and compassionate, both with yourself and with others.

Questions to ask yourself:

- How can I respond in a way that aligns with my values rather than react impulsively?

- What is the most mindful and respectful way to address this situation?

- What can I do to calm my mind and body in this moment before responding?

4. **Embracing:** After the moment has passed, reflect on the lesson it offers. What did you learn about yourself? How can this situation

help you grow? Embrace the experience as part of your healing journey.

Questions to ask yourself:

- What did this situation teach me about my emotional patterns or triggers?
- How can I use this experience to grow and strengthen my self-awareness?
- How can I embrace this moment as part of my journey toward greater emotional resilience?

Real-Life Example: Managing a Triggering Situation with Inner Dialogue

Let's look at how inner dialogue can play out in a real-life situation, using the HOME Method to guide the process.

Story: A Conflict with a Close Friend

Nicole was out to dinner with her friend Lena when a small disagreement over where to eat escalated into an argument. Lena criticized Nicole's choice of restaurant, and Nicole felt a familiar surge of anger and hurt. In the past, she might have reacted defensively, saying something she didn't mean or shutting down to avoid the confrontation. But this time, Nicole decided to apply the HOME Method through inner dialogue.

- **Healing:** As soon as Nicole felt triggered, she paused and reminded herself that this moment was an opportunity for healing. She realized the argument wasn't really about the restaurant—it was tapping into her deep-seated fear of not being respected, something she had struggled with since childhood.

- o **Nicole's inner dialogue:** "Why am I feeling so upset? Is this really about the restaurant, or is it bringing up an old feeling of being disrespected? How can I use this to understand my fear of being dismissed?"

- **Observing:** Nicole asked herself, "Why am I feeling so upset about this minor disagreement?" As she reflected, she recognized that her reaction was rooted in past experiences where her opinions were dismissed. Instead of reacting to the situation impulsively, she observed how her body felt tense and how her thoughts spiraled toward feeling unappreciated.

  - o **Nicole's inner dialogue:** "I notice my heart racing, and I feel tense. I've felt this way before when I thought someone didn't value my opinion. I can see this isn't just about Lena—it's about how I've felt dismissed in the past."

- **Mindfulness:** After observing her emotional state, Nicole responded mindfully. She said, "Lena, I'm feeling upset, but I think it's more about me than this conversation. Can we pause for a moment?" By doing this, Nicole prevented the situation from escalating and created space for herself to process her feelings.

  - o **Nicole's inner dialogue:** "I need to take a breath and address this calmly. This isn't just about this moment, and I don't want to react impulsively. How can I speak to Lena in a way that honors both my feelings and hers?"

- **Embracing:** Once Nicole had calmed down, she reflected on what the disagreement had taught her. She embraced the lesson that her feelings of being disrespected were rooted in old patterns and acknowledged the importance of addressing these triggers with self-awareness moving forward.

  o **Nicole's inner dialogue:** "I can see now that this situation taught me about my fear of being dismissed. How can I work on this pattern moving forward? What can I learn from this about setting boundaries and communicating my needs?"

How Inner Dialogue Transforms Triggering Situations

What Nicole did during the dinner was turn a potentially painful moment into an opportunity for self-reflection and emotional growth. By engaging in inner dialogue and applying the HOME Method, she was able to recognize the deeper issue behind her reaction and make a conscious decision to handle the situation differently. This not only helped her avoid unnecessary conflict but also deepened her understanding of her emotional landscape.

When you engage in inner dialogue during a triggering situation, you allow yourself to:

- **Unpack Complex Emotions:** Instead of being swept away by intense emotions, inner dialogue helps you break them down into manageable pieces. You can begin to understand why you feel the way you do without getting overwhelmed.

- **Create Space Between Trigger and Reaction:** Pausing to ask yourself compassionate questions provides emotional distance, giving you the opportunity to choose your response rather than react impulsively.

- **See Patterns in Real Time:** By observing your reactions, you can begin to notice emotional patterns that have been repeating over time. Inner dialogue reveals these patterns as they happen, giving you a chance to change them.

Developing Your Inner Dialogue Practice

As you begin to develop your own practice of inner dialogue, remember that it's not about achieving perfection. Instead, it's about being present with yourself in the moments when you're feeling most vulnerable. Here's how you can begin to integrate inner dialogue with the HOME Method into your daily life:

1. **Recognize Your Emotional Triggers:** When you feel a surge of emotion, pause and recognize that you're being triggered. Take this as a signal that something deeper is going on.

   Questions to ask yourself:
   - What is this trigger revealing about my emotional state?
   - Where do I feel this reaction in my body?
   - Am I reacting to the present moment, or is this bringing up something from my past?

2. **Ask Compassionate Questions:** Start the inner dialogue by asking yourself questions like, "What am I feeling? Where is this emotion coming from? Is this really about the current situation, or is it tied to something else?"

   Questions to ask yourself:
   - What am I feeling right now, and why?
   - Where is this emotion really coming from?
   - How can I approach this situation with curiosity rather than judgment?

3. **Observe Without Judgment:** Take a few moments to observe your emotions. Notice where you feel them in your body and what thoughts are coming up. Stay curious, not judgmental.

   Questions to ask yourself:
   - What am I noticing about my physical and emotional reactions?
   - Am I being hard on myself for feeling this way?
   - How can I observe this situation without jumping to conclusions?

4. **Respond Mindfully:** Once you've taken the time to reflect, respond to the situation mindfully. This may mean addressing the situation calmly, taking a break, or deciding not to engage at all.

   Questions to ask yourself:
   - What's the most thoughtful and mindful way to address this situation?

- o How can I respond without letting my emotions take over?
- o What response would feel most aligned with my true self?

5. **Embrace the Lesson:** After the moment has passed, reflect on what the situation taught you. What did you learn about yourself? How can this experience help you grow?

Questions to ask yourself:

- o What can I learn from this experience about my emotional triggers?
- o How can I use this lesson to navigate similar situations in the future?
- o How can I embrace this experience as part of my personal growth?

Affirmations for Practicing Inner Dialogue

Here are some affirmations to help you strengthen your inner dialogue practice:

1. I pause and listen to myself with compassion and curiosity.
2. I recognize that every emotional reaction is an opportunity for healing.
3. I create space between my emotions and my response.
4. I approach my emotions with kindness, knowing they are part of my journey.
5. I respond mindfully, not impulsively, to difficult situations.
6. I am learning from my emotional experiences growing stronger each day.
7. I embrace the lessons that each emotional trigger brings me.

Chapter 8

The Quest for the Real You: Unveiling Your Authentic Self

Introduction: The Journey to the Authentic Self

For much of my life, I believed that my purpose was to meet the expectations of others—whether those of my family, society, or even the image I had of myself. I wore the identities I thought would earn approval, success, and, above all, acceptance. I learned from a young age to hide my true feelings and to silence my desires. My childhood was a breeding ground for the idea that survival meant fitting into a mold, and for years, I did just that.

But as I moved through adulthood, something began to shift. Despite outward success, I felt a deep disconnection from myself. There was an emptiness I couldn't explain, and no amount of external achievement could fill it. I remember vividly sitting in my office, looking out the window, wondering why I felt so far away from the life I had imagined. That was the first clue that I wasn't living my truth.

The journey to find my authentic self wasn't sudden—it was gradual, full of setbacks and revelations. The masks I had worn for so long had become so comfortable that taking them off felt terrifying. But beneath them, there was a person waiting to emerge. The more I embraced my true self, the more I realized that discovering who we really are is not a destination but an ongoing journey. Over time, as we heal and grow, our understanding of ourselves deepens and evolves. The beauty of the journey is that it is dynamic—our authentic self shifts and unfolds as we peel away layers of conditioning and trauma.

Affirmation: I am committed to uncovering and living as my true self, free from the masks and conditioning that no longer serve me.

Peeling Back the Layers: Understanding Conditioning and Social Programming Conditioning begins early. As children, we are like sponges, absorbing the expectations of those around us—our parents, our teachers, and society at large. In my family, success wasn't just encouraged. It was required. Achievement meant worthiness, and anything less than perfection felt like failure. I internalized this belief, and it shaped every decision I made.

In my teenage years, this conditioning intensified. I remember constantly striving for approval, not because I truly enjoyed what I was doing, but because I believed that it was the only way to feel valuable. Whether it was academic achievements, professional goals, or even relationships, I found myself playing roles that weren't aligned with who I was.

However, societal conditioning is not just about family expectations. It's also shaped by culture, religion, and media. From a young age, we are bombarded with images of success, beauty, and happiness. We are told that to be happy, we must look a certain way, earn a certain amount of money, or have a certain lifestyle. These messages can be so powerful that we begin to believe they are our desires when, in reality, they have little to do with who we are at our core.

I vividly remember a turning point when I realized that much of what I had been striving for wasn't even mine. I had been chasing someone else's version of happiness. When I looked at my life closely, I saw how much of it had been shaped by outside forces. This realization was painful, but it was also the first step toward liberation.

The Beauty of Change: Evolving Identities

What's fascinating is that as I began to unpack these layers, I also realized that who I thought I was had been in flux all along. The person I believed myself to be—driven by the need for external validation—began to fade away as I healed. In the beginning, it felt as though I was losing my sense of self, but over time, I came to understand that my identity was not fixed. It evolved as I matured, as I healed the wounds of my past, and as I embraced new aspects of myself.

What I discovered is that identity isn't static. We may think we know who we are, but as we grow, heal, and uncover deeper layers, our sense of self naturally changes. And that's part of the beauty of this journey. Each time we peel back another layer of conditioning or heal an old wound, we get closer to the core of who we are—but that core may look different today than it did yesterday. There's freedom in knowing that we don't have to be rigid in our understanding of ourselves.

I've come to believe that our authentic self is always in motion, always evolving. The person I am today is more aligned with my truth than the person I was ten years ago—and ten years from now, I may have a deeper understanding of who I am. The key is to embrace this change, to know that finding your true self is not a one-time discovery but an ongoing process of growth and transformation.

Affirmation: I release the beliefs and expectations placed on me by others. I am free to live life on my terms.

Affirmation: I trust that my true self is enough and worthy of love, just as I am.

Identifying Your Core Values and True Desires

One of the most challenging yet rewarding parts of my journey was discovering my core values. After years of living in a way that felt inauthentic, I had lost touch with what really mattered to me. I remember sitting down with a journal and asking myself the simple yet powerful question: What do I truly value?

At first, the answers were clouded by years of societal conditioning. I thought I valued success, prestige, and security. But as I dug deeper, I began to realize that these were values I had inherited, not ones that resonated with my true self. What I actually valued were freedom, creativity, and deep connections with others.

Evolving Values and Desires

What's important to understand is that our values, much like our identities, can shift and evolve over time. As I matured and healed, I realized that some of the things I once thought were core to my identity no longer felt true. For example, I used to place a great deal of value on achievement and external success, but as I healed, I found that these values no longer resonated with me.

Instead, I began to value inner peace, creativity, and authentic connections.

This shift wasn't immediate—it unfolded slowly as I let go of the old beliefs that had been guiding my life. As I learned more about who I was, I allowed my values and desires to change. I gave myself permission to let go of the things that no longer served me, even if they had once felt essential to my identity.

If you feel like your values are shifting or evolving as you grow, know that this is entirely normal. It's a sign that you are coming into deeper alignment with your true self. The key is to remain open to change and to allow yourself to evolve. Our values are not fixed; they are reflections of where we are on our journey. As we heal and grow, our values and desires will naturally shift to reflect the person we are becoming.

Affirmation: I am guided by my core values of [insert your core values here], and I honor them in every decision I make.

Affirmation: My desires are valid, and I permit myself to pursue what truly brings me joy.

The Masks We Wear: Letting Go of Societal Conditioning

The masks we wear are often put on in response to early trauma or emotional neglect. For me, the mask of the "overachiever" was a survival mechanism. If I could just achieve enough, I thought, I would finally be worthy of love and acceptance. But over time, the mask became suffocating.

In my professional life, I was known as someone who could handle anything. I took pride in being the "fixer," the person who could step in and solve problems. But inside, I was crumbling. The pressure to maintain this image took a toll on my mental and emotional health. I felt like a fraud, constantly afraid that if people saw the real me, they would reject me.

The Fear of Shedding Masks

Taking off that mask was one of the hardest things I've ever done. It meant admitting that I wasn't perfect, that I didn't have it all together, and that I needed help. But once I began to show up as my authentic self, I found that the people who mattered the most—those who loved me for me—accepted me more fully than I had ever imagined.

However, there was also fear involved in shedding the masks. The truth is, these masks become like armor. We wear them to protect ourselves from pain, rejection, and judgment. Taking them off can feel vulnerable and raw. There were moments when I worried that without my mask of perfection, people would see me as weak or unworthy. But the opposite was true. The more I let go of the need to appear perfect, the more authentic and meaningful my connections became.

What I've come to realize is that the masks we wear may feel safe, but they keep us disconnected from others—and from ourselves. They prevent us from experiencing real intimacy and authenticity. The process of letting go of these masks is uncomfortable, but it's essential if we want to live authentically.

Affirmation: I release the need to be perfect. I am allowed to show up exactly as I am. Affirmation: I choose to remove the masks I've worn to fit in and embrace my authentic self. The Mirror Effect: **Relationships as Reflections of Your Authentic Self.**

In a previous chapter, we discussed how relationships act as mirrors, and as I began to embrace my authentic self, I noticed a shift in my relationships. As a result of my newfound authenticity, I was attracting people into my life. We see ourselves reflected back to us through our relationships.

In the past, when I was wearing masks and living according to others' expectations, my relationships reflected that. I often found myself in friendships and partnerships where I didn't feel truly seen or valued. These relationships mirrored the parts of myself that I had not yet healed. They showed me where I was still seeking external validation or where I was afraid to show up as my true self.

As I began to heal and embrace my authentic self, the dynamics in my relationships changed. I started attracting people who valued me for who I was, not for what I could do or achieve. I noticed that my connections became deeper, more meaningful, and more aligned with my true values.

The mirror effect works both ways. As we discover more of ourselves, our relationships begin to reflect that newfound authenticity. The people in our lives become clearer mirrors, reflecting back the parts of us that are aligned with our truth. But it's important to recognize that this process may also reveal where certain relationships no longer serve us. As we grow, we may outgrow relationships that were built on inauthenticity or shared trauma. Letting go of these relationships can be painful, but it's a necessary part of the journey.

Affirmation: As I discover my authentic self, I attract relationships that reflect my truth and values.

Affirmation: I release relationships that no longer serve my growth and embrace connections that support my authentic journey.

Practical Exercises for Uncovering Your Authentic Self

Journaling became a key part of my healing process. I started with simple prompts: What brings me joy? When do I feel most like myself? These questions helped me peel back the layers and get to the heart of who I was. Over time, I began to notice patterns in my responses. I felt most alive when I was being creative, when I was connecting with others on a deep level, and when I was engaged in activities that aligned with my values.

Another powerful tool was mindfulness. Through meditation, I learned to quiet the external noise and listen to my inner voice. This practice helped me differentiate between my conditioned thoughts and my true desires.

 Finally, I began a daily practice of checking in with myself. Each evening, I would ask: Did I live in alignment with my values today? If the answer was no, I didn't beat myself up about it.

Instead, I reflected on what had pulled me out of alignment and made a plan to do better the next day.

Affirmation: Each day, I come closer to living as my true self, honoring my values, and listening to my inner voice.

Affirmation: I have the courage to be authentic, even when it feels uncomfortable.

Exercise: Writing a Personal Mission Statement

Writing a personal mission statement was a transformative experience for me. It forced me to get clear on what mattered most and to create a roadmap for how I wanted to live my life. My mission statement became my compass, guiding me through difficult decisions and reminding me of my core values.

To create your own mission statement, start by reflecting on your values and what gives your life meaning. Write down the words or phrases that resonate most deeply with you. Then, combine them into a simple, clear statement that reflects how you want to show up in the world.

My personal mission statement reads: I am committed to living a life of authenticity, creative expression, and compassionate connection. I will pursue my passions with integrity and embrace all parts of myself, knowing that I am enough just as I am.

Affirmation: I am clear about my purpose, and I use my personal mission statement as a guide to living authentically.

Affirmation: I honor my truth and commit to living in alignment with my values and desires.

Chapter 9

Healing Waters: Diving Deep into Emotional Renewal

Introduction: The Nature of Healing

Healing is often described as a journey, but what we don't always acknowledge is how non-linear that journey can be. There are moments when we feel like we've made incredible progress, only to find ourselves revisiting old wounds we thought we had already healed. This is the nature of emotional renewal—it isn't a straight path but a cycle that brings us deeper into our own hearts with each turn.

In my own life, I've found that healing is rarely a one-time event. It's a process that unfolds in waves, where each layer we peel back reveals something new. At times, it can feel overwhelming to revisit the same emotional terrain, but I've come to understand that this is not a sign of failure—it's a sign of deeper healing. The more we allow ourselves to dive into these emotional waters, the more we uncover, release, and renew.

This chapter is about exploring the nature of emotional healing and renewal. It's about understanding that healing is not about "fixing" ourselves but about creating space for our emotions to move, flow, and ultimately transform us. Emotional renewal is the process of allowing ourselves to rest, reflect, and emerge with a deeper sense of clarity and peace.

Affirmation: I trust the process of healing, knowing that it unfolds in its own time.

Understanding the Healing Process

We all carry emotional wounds from the past. Some of these wounds are obvious, the result of major traumas or painful experiences. Others are more subtle, shaped by years of unmet needs, unexpressed emotions, or beliefs we've internalized about ourselves. Regardless of how they originated, these emotional wounds often linger beneath the surface, affecting how we interact with ourselves and others.

One of the most profound realizations I had on my healing journey was that the process of healing doesn't happen all at once. It happens in layers. At first, I thought that once I had addressed a particular wound, it would be "healed" forever. But I soon discovered that healing is cyclical. As we grow, new layers of our wounds reveal themselves, often in response to life's challenges.

This isn't a sign that we haven't healed—it's a sign that we're ready to go deeper. Each time we revisit an old wound, we bring new awareness and wisdom to it. This deeper understanding

allows us to heal the wound in a more profound way. For me, this process of returning to old wounds felt frustrating at times, but I came to realize that each layer of healing was necessary for my emotional renewal.

Affirmation: I allow myself to heal in layers, knowing that each return to old wounds brings new wisdom.

Techniques for Emotional Healing

Healing can take many forms, and the path to emotional renewal is unique for everyone. Over the years, I've explored a variety of healing techniques that have supported my emotional growth and transformation. What I've learned is that healing isn't about "doing" something specific—it's about creating space for your emotions to be felt, processed, and released.

Here are some techniques that I've found to be particularly powerful:

- **Journaling for Emotional Processing**: Writing has always been a therapeutic outlet for me. When emotions feel overwhelming or unclear, I turn to my journal to process what I'm feeling. Sometimes, just putting my thoughts on paper helps me untangle the knot of emotions inside. I've used journaling not just as a way to vent but as a way to reflect, explore, and understand the deeper roots of my emotions.

  Exercise: Try journaling for ten minutes each day, focusing on a specific emotion that has been lingering. Write without judgment or censorship, allowing whatever comes up to flow freely. Afterward, reflect on any patterns or insights that arise.

- **Mindfulness and Meditation for Emotional Clarity:** One of the most transformative practices for me has been mindfulness meditation. When I feel emotionally overwhelmed, I use meditation as a way to ground myself and create space between my emotions and my reactions. By simply sitting with my emotions and observing them without trying to change or fix them, I've found that they begin to shift naturally.

Exercise: Try a ten-minute mindfulness meditation focused on your breath. As you breathe in, notice any emotions that are present without labeling them. As you breathe out, imagine those emotions gently flowing out of your body like water.

- **Therapy and Breathwork for Deeper Healing:** Professional support has been a critical part of my healing journey. Therapy, particularly talk therapy and body-focused therapies like breathwork, has allowed me to dive deeper into my emotions and release stored trauma. Breathwork, in particular, has been a powerful tool for releasing stuck emotions from my body. By focusing on the breath, I've been able to move through emotional blockages that words alone couldn't release.

  Affirmation: I create space for my emotions to flow freely and trust in the healing process.

The Cyclical Nature of Healing

One of the most challenging aspects of healing is the feeling of revisiting the same issues over and over again. At times, it can feel as though we're stuck in a loop—dealing with the same wounds, the same emotional triggers, the same patterns. But what I've come to understand is that healing is not linear. It's cyclical, much like the seasons of nature.

Just as the earth goes through cycles of growth, decay, rest, and renewal, so too do our emotions. There will be periods where everything feels in bloom, where we feel energized, healed, and whole. And there will be times when old wounds resurface when we feel tired, raw, or even broken. These periods of emotional decay are not failures—they are opportunities for more profound healing.

In my own life, I've returned to the same emotional wounds many times. Early on in my journey, I felt frustrated by this. I believed that if I had truly healed, I wouldn't need to revisit these wounds. But what I've learned is that each time I revisit a wound, I bring new insight and healing to it. What once felt like a debilitating emotional pattern now feels like an invitation to go deeper into my own heart.

The cycles of healing are necessary for emotional renewal. Just as nature needs time to rest and renew, so do we. Allow yourself to embrace the cyclical nature of healing. Trust that each return to an old wound brings you closer to wholeness, even if it feels repetitive in the moment.

Affirmation: I honor the cyclical nature of healing and trust that each return to old wounds brings deeper renewal.

Self-Care as a Tool for Emotional Renewal

One of the most important lessons I've learned in my healing journey is the power of self-care. True healing doesn't just happen in the moments when we're actively processing our emotions—it happens in the quiet moments of rest, play, and nurturing ourselves. Self-care is the foundation of emotional renewal. It's what allows us to integrate the emotional work we've done and emerge feeling whole again.

For me, self-care has taken many forms. Some days, it looks like taking a long walk in nature, allowing the beauty of the world around me to soothe my spirit. Other days, it's a quiet evening with a good TV show or a movie, giving myself permission to rest and recharge. There have also been times when self-care meant setting boundaries—learning to say no to commitments that drained me and yes to the things that nourished me.

Affirmation: I nurture myself with rest, creativity, and care, knowing that self-care is an essential part of emotional renewal.

Creating Your Personal Healing Plan

Healing is deeply personal, and no two journeys are the same. That's why creating your own personal healing plan can be a powerful way to stay connected to your process of emotional renewal. A healing plan is a roadmap that guides you through the emotional work you need to do while also ensuring that you are taking time for self-care and rest.

In creating your personal healing plan, consider the following elements:

- **What wounds need healing:** Reflect on the emotional wounds that are still present in your life. Are there patterns that keep repeating? Are there emotions you've been avoiding? Identify the areas where deeper healing is needed.

- **What healing techniques work for you:** Think about the techniques that have been most effective in your healing journey. Is it journaling, meditation, therapy, or something else? Incorporate these techniques into your plan.

- **How you will nurture yourself:** Healing requires energy, so it's important to include self-care in your plan. Make a list of self-care activities that nourish you, and commit to incorporating them into your daily life.

Affirmation: I commit to my healing journey and honor the time it takes to renew emotionally.

Chapter 10

The Silent Witness: Mastering the Art of Observing Without Judgment

Introduction: The Power of Observation

At the heart of true self-awareness lies the ability to observe our inner world without judgment.

This may sound simple, but it's one of the most challenging things we can practice. Our minds are naturally wired to analyze, critique, and form judgments about ourselves and our experiences. Yet, healing often requires us to step back and observe without immediately rushing to label what we see as "good" or "bad."

This is where the concept of the "silent witness" comes in. The silent witness is the part of you that watches, notices, and holds space for all of your emotions, thoughts, and experiences without getting tangled in them. When we tap into this silent witness, we allow ourselves to observe our inner world without criticism, creating the room we need to grow, heal, and transform.

When I first encountered the idea of non-judgmental observation, I was skeptical. How could I not judge what was happening inside me? I was so accustomed to analyzing every thought and feeling, picking it apart to understand it better or to fix it. But over time, I realized that judgment was holding me back. It was keeping me stuck in loops of guilt, shame, and anxiety.

Instead of helping me understand myself better, judgment created a barrier between me and my true feelings.

When we observe without judgment, we create space for compassion, understanding, and deep emotional healing. We begin to see ourselves with greater clarity, not as a collection of mistakes or flaws, but as whole and evolving beings. The silent witness is the part of us that can sit with discomfort, uncertainty, and pain and know that it is all part of the human experience.

In this chapter, we'll explore how to cultivate the silent witness within, how to detach from judgment, and how this practice leads to greater inner peace. By mastering the art of observing without judgment, you'll learn to free yourself from the cycles of self-criticism and emotional turmoil.

Affirmation: I am a compassionate observer of my thoughts and emotions, allowing them to flow without judgment.

The Mind as a Critic: Recognizing Self-Judgment

For most of us, the mind is often a harsh critic. It judges our thoughts, actions, and emotions, labeling them as "right" or "wrong," "good" or "bad." How many times have you caught yourself thinking, I shouldn't feel this way, or Why did I do that? These judgments can trap us in cycles of shame, guilt, or frustration.

I've experienced this firsthand. For years, my mind was my harshest critic. I would criticize myself for feeling emotions I thought were "weak" or "unacceptable." When I felt anger, my mind would immediately jump to self-judgment: I shouldn't be angry. What's wrong with me? This inner dialogue only deepened my emotional turmoil and created more layers of guilt and shame that took years to unravel.

We live in a society that teaches us to evaluate everything—including our feelings. From a young age, we are taught which emotions are "appropriate" and which ones should be avoided. As a result, we internalize the belief that some emotions are bad or wrong, and we begin to judge ourselves harshly when we experience them. This leads to a pattern of repressing emotions or feeling ashamed of them, which prevents us from healing and moving forward.

What I've learned is that self-judgment doesn't serve us. It doesn't help us process our emotions or grow. Instead, it keeps us stuck in patterns of self-criticism and emotional suppression. When we judge ourselves, we close the door to compassion, which is the key to healing.

The first step in breaking this cycle of self-judgment is recognizing it. When you notice yourself judging your emotions—whether it's anger, sadness, fear, or even joy—pause and observe the judgment. Instead of engaging with it, simply notice that it's there. This act of noticing creates a space between you and the judgment, allowing you to choose a different response.

Personal story: I remember a time when I was overwhelmed with anxiety. My mind was racing, and I felt trapped in my thoughts. Instead of allowing myself to feel the anxiety, I began to judge it. I shouldn't be feeling this way. What's wrong with me? But as I observed this self-judgment, I realized that the anxiety was simply a signal that I needed to slow down and take care of myself. By observing the judgment without engaging with it, I was able to shift from criticism to compassion.

Affirmation: I release the need to judge myself or my emotions. I allow myself to simply observe.

Becoming the Silent Witness: Observing Without Judgment

Cultivating the "silent witness" takes practice, but it's one of the most powerful tools for personal transformation. The silent witness is the part of you that can watch your thoughts and emotions from a place of calm awareness. It doesn't try to fix, change, or label—it simply observes.

You don't need to force yourself to feel differently or rush to fix what you think is wrong. In fact, one of the keys to healing is allowing yourself to sit with your feelings just as they are without trying to alter them. This is where observation, as we discussed in the HOME method, becomes essential. By observing without judgment, you gain insight into your true self.

A Reminder of the HOME Method: The Observation step is a powerful tool for staying present with your emotions. It's important to remember that mindfulness doesn't always look like sitting in meditation. Sometimes, mindfulness is what you practice when you're in the middle of a heated conversation or feeling overwhelmed by stress. You can go "HOME" by stepping into that observer role, noticing your emotions as they arise, and acknowledging them without reacting.

For example, if you're in an argument, instead of reacting impulsively, pause and observe: What am I feeling right now? What thoughts are rushing through my mind? This act of observation creates a buffer, giving you the space to respond more thoughtfully instead of from a place of reactivity.

Techniques for Cultivating the Silent Witness:

Mindful Breathing: One of the simplest ways to access the silent witness is through mindful breathing. When you focus on your breath, you anchor yourself in the present moment, allowing your thoughts to come and go without attaching to them.

Exercise: When you notice judgment arising, take a few deep breaths. Focus on the sensation of the air entering and leaving your body. Allow the judgment to pass without engaging with it.

Body Awareness: Bringing awareness to your body can help you stay grounded in the present. Often, our emotions manifest as physical sensations—tightness in the chest, a knot in the stomach, or tension in the shoulders.

Exercise: When you feel overwhelmed by emotion, take a moment to scan your body. Notice where you're holding tension. Breathe into those areas and simply observe the sensations without trying to change them.

Non-Reactive Listening: Another way to cultivate the silent witness is through non-reactive listening, both to yourself and others. When someone is speaking to you, practice listening without forming judgments or preparing your response. This can help you stay present and deepen your connections.

Exercise: The next time someone speaks to you, focus entirely on their words. Notice any judgments or reactions that arise, but don't act on them. Simply observe them and return to listening.

Affirmation: I step into the role of the silent witness, observing my thoughts and emotions with calm awareness.

The Freedom of Non-Judgmental Awareness

When we practice observing without judgment, we open the door to a new kind of freedom.

Non-judgmental awareness allows us to see our thoughts and emotions for what they are: passing experiences that don't define us. It gives us the space to feel our emotions fully without getting stuck in them.

Judgment keeps us in a state of tension, where we are constantly evaluating ourselves and trying to measure up to an impossible standard. When we let go of judgment, we release that tension and allow ourselves to be present with what is. This doesn't mean we ignore our emotions or pretend that everything is fine—it means we approach our emotions with curiosity and compassion rather than criticism.

Examples of how judgment hinders healing:

When we judge our sadness, we resist feeling it fully, which prolongs the healing process. When we judge our anger, we suppress it, only for it to resurface later in more destructive ways. When we judge our joy, we diminish its power and rob ourselves of the full experience of happiness.

By releasing judgment, we create space for all of our emotions to be felt and processed in a healthy way. This leads to deeper self-understanding and greater emotional resilience.

Affirmation: I release judgment and allow myself to experience the freedom of non-judgmental awareness.

Integrating Observation into Daily Life

Practicing non-judgmental observation isn't just something you do during meditation or quiet moments of reflection. It's something you can bring into every aspect of your life. Whether you're going through a stressful day at work, dealing with a difficult conversation, or even performing mundane tasks like washing the dishes, you can practice observing without judgment.

Mindfulness in Daily Tasks: One of the easiest ways to integrate observation into daily life is by bringing mindfulness into the tasks you normally do on autopilot. For example, when you're washing the dishes, instead of letting your mind wander to your to-do list or replaying a conversation from earlier in the day, focus on the sensations of the water, the sound of the dishes, and the movement of your hands. This simple act of observation brings you into the present moment and allows you to experience the task with greater awareness.

Shifting from Reactive to Reflective Living: One of the greatest gifts of cultivating the silent witness is that it allows you to shift from being reactive to being reflective. Instead of immediately reacting to a situation or emotion, you can pause, observe, and respond from a place of calm awareness.

Exercise: The next time you find yourself in a stressful situation, practice creating a "pause" before reacting. Take a deep breath, observe your thoughts and feelings, and choose a response that aligns with your values and goals.

Affirmation: I integrate non-judgmental observation into my daily life, creating space for mindfulness and compassion.

Exercise: Daily Observation Practice

To help you cultivate the practice of observing without judgment, here's a simple daily observation exercise:

1. **Set Aside 10 Minutes:** Each day, set aside 10 minutes for a practice of non-judgmental observation. Find a quiet space where you won't be interrupted.

2. **Observe Your Thoughts:** Close your eyes and begin to observe your thoughts. Notice what arises without labeling it as good or bad. Simply observe the flow of thoughts without getting attached to them.

3. **Notice Emotions and Sensations:** Shift your attention to your body. Notice any physical sensations, such as tension or relaxation. Observe your emotions as they arise without trying to change them.

4. **Write Down Your Observations:** After your practice, take a few minutes to write down what you observed. Notice any patterns in your thoughts or emotions, and reflect on how you can bring more non-judgmental awareness into your day.

This simple practice, done consistently, will help you develop the habit of observing without judgment, allowing you to navigate life's challenges with greater ease and compassion.

Chapter 11
Embracing Change—Finding Growth in Transformation

Introduction: The Constant of Change

Change is one of the few constants in life. It comes whether we ask for it or not, reshaping our circumstances, our perspectives, and sometimes even who we are. Whether it's a shift in our external world—a new job, the end of a relationship, moving to a new place—or internal changes like personal growth, emotional healing, or shifting beliefs, change is inevitable.

Yet, for many of us, change brings discomfort and fear. We resist it, holding on tightly to what is familiar, even if it no longer serves us. But what if we could learn to embrace change as an essential part of life, something that moves us toward our true selves? What if, instead of fearing change, we welcomed it as an opportunity for growth and transformation?

In this chapter, we'll explore how the HOME Method—Healing, Observing, Mindfulness, and Embracing—can help you navigate change with grace and openness. You'll discover how to let go of the need for control, lean into uncertainty, and allow change to become a powerful catalyst for your personal evolution.

Why We Resist Change

Before we explore how to embrace change, it's important to understand why we so often resist it. Resistance to change is deeply rooted in fear. We fear the unknown, the loss of control, and the possibility that change might bring discomfort or pain. Even when we know that a particular change is necessary or beneficial, there's a part of us that clings to the familiar because it feels safer.

On a deeper level, our resistance to change can be tied to past wounds. If you've experienced loss, rejection, or trauma, change might stir up old fears, reminding you of times when you felt unsafe or unsteady. This emotional response can make change feel threatening, even when it's positive or necessary.

Story: My Fear of Letting Go

For much of my life, I resisted change, especially when it came to relationships. I stayed in friendships and partnerships that no longer served me because the idea of letting go felt too risky. I was afraid of being alone, of losing my sense of identity, and of the uncertainty that came with stepping into the unknown.

Even when I knew, deep down, that certain relationships were holding me back, I clung to them out of fear. It wasn't until I started confronting this fear and accepting that change was part of my growth that I was able to move forward. Letting go became a necessary part of my healing process, and though it was difficult, it opened up space for healthier, more fulfilling connections.

The Role of Healing in Embracing Change

The first step in embracing change is understanding that it's a crucial part of your healing journey. Change, especially when it feels uncomfortable, offers you the opportunity to address unresolved emotions, old beliefs, and unhealed wounds. When we resist change, we're often resisting the healing that it can bring.

Healing requires us to shed layers of our old selves—identities, beliefs, or patterns that no longer serve us. These layers might have protected us in the past, but as we grow, they can keep us stuck. Change allows us to release these layers and step into a more authentic version of ourselves.

Story: Taking a Leap of Faith and Moving to a New Country

In my early 20s, I took the biggest leap of faith in my life. My heart was shattered by grief and depression after my sister committed suicide. My emotions were raw, and I knew instinctively that I needed a radical change to overcome the darkness I was in. Moving to a country I had never been to before felt terrifying. I had no guarantees, no safety net, and I was deeply afraid of the unknown.

I remember standing at the airport, terrified yet knowing that this was something I had to do. The fear was overwhelming, but so was my need for change. I didn't fully understand it at the time, but this move was my way of saving myself from the deep despair I felt. Nearly 30 years later, I can look back and say that this was the best decision I ever made. That change—so terrifying in the moment— opened the door to healing and growth I couldn't have imagined.

What I learned from that experience is that sometimes, the most profound healing comes when we embrace the changes we're most afraid of. In stepping into the unknown, I found not only a new life but also a deeper connection to myself. Change, though uncomfortable, became my path to transformation.

Observing Change Without Judgment

One of the most challenging aspects of change is the emotions it stirs up. You might feel excitement one moment and fear the next. You may swing between hope and doubt. It's natural to feel conflicted during times of transition, but when you judge these emotions—labeling them as "bad" or "wrong"—you create more resistance.

The next step in embracing change is to observe it without judgment. This means allowing yourself to experience the full range of emotions that come with change and recognizing them as part of the process. Instead of categorizing change as "good" or "bad," simply observe how it unfolds, knowing that it's leading you to growth.

Story: Observing My Emotional Rollercoaster During a Move

When I moved to a new country for a fresh start, I was excited about the possibilities. But as the moving date approached, I started to feel overwhelmed by doubt and anxiety. Every day, my emotions seemed to shift. One day, I'd be excited about the new adventure; the next, I'd feel terrified and unsure if I'd made the right choice.

Rather than judging these emotions or letting them dictate my decisions, I began to simply observe them. I reminded myself that it was okay to feel scared and uncertain. I allowed myself to feel the full spectrum of emotions without labeling them as "wrong" or "bad." This practice of observation helped me move through the change without getting stuck in my fears.

Mindfulness: Staying Grounded in the Midst of Change

Mindfulness is a powerful tool for staying present during times of change. When life shifts—whether unexpectedly or by choice—it's easy to become lost in "what ifs" and worst-case scenarios. Our minds naturally drift into the future, trying to predict what will happen or into the past, clinging to what we're leaving behind.

By practicing mindfulness, you can ground yourself in the present moment, even when everything else feels uncertain. Mindfulness helps you stay connected to yourself as you navigate change, allowing you to respond with intention instead of reacting out of fear.

Story: Using Mindfulness to Navigate Relationship Changes

One of the most significant changes I faced was the end of a long-term relationship. As the relationship ended, my mind constantly raced with thoughts about the future—Would I ever find love again? What if I stayed single forever? What would life look like without this person?

These thoughts were overwhelming, but through mindfulness, I learned to bring myself back to the present. I practiced staying grounded in each moment rather than getting lost in the fear of what might happen next. I focused on small, simple actions that helped me feel connected to the present—whether it was taking a mindful walk, focusing on my breath, or journaling about how I felt at that moment.

Mindfulness helped me realize that even though the future was uncertain, I didn't have to figure it all out right away. I could trust myself to handle each moment as it came.

Embracing Change as a Path to Growth

The final step in navigating change is to fully embrace it. Embracing change means accepting it as part of life's natural flow and trusting that it's leading you toward growth. Even when change feels uncomfortable or scary, leaning into it allows you to evolve, discover new parts of yourself, and expand your sense of what's possible.

Embracing change doesn't mean that you'll never feel fear or resistance—it means that you choose to move forward despite those feelings. It's about trusting that the discomfort of change is temporary, and on the other side of it lies transformation.

Story: Embracing My Identity After Major Life Changes

After a series of life-altering events, including a career change, the end of a relationship, and a move to a new country, I found myself feeling like I didn't recognize my life. Everything had shifted, and I no longer knew who I was without the roles and routines that had defined me for so long.

At first, I resisted this change. I tried to hold onto my old identity, the version of myself that fit neatly into the life I used to live. But the more I tried to cling to the past, the more stuck I felt. It wasn't until I made the conscious decision to embrace the changes in my life that I began to feel free again.

By embracing change, I gave myself permission to evolve. I allowed myself to discover new aspects of my identity, to try new things, and to let go of the old roles that no longer fit. This act of embracing change was liberating—it opened the door to growth in ways I never could have imagined.

Exercise: Embracing Change with the HOME Method

To practice embracing change in your life, try the following exercise using the HOME Method:

1. **Healing**: Identify a change you're currently experiencing or anticipating. Ask yourself, "What old patterns or beliefs is this change asking me to heal?" Write down any fears or resistance you feel and reflect on how this change is part of your healing journey.

2. **Observing:** Take a moment to observe your emotions around this change without judgment. What are you feeling, and where do you feel it in your body? Simply notice your thoughts and feelings without trying to change or fix them.

3. **Mindfulness:** Practice mindfulness by grounding yourself in the present moment. Focus on your breath, noticing how each inhale and exhale feels. Allow yourself to stay in the present without worrying about the future or dwelling on the past.

4.   **Embracing:** Write down three things about this change that you are willing to embrace. How can this change help you grow? What new opportunities or perspectives is it offering you? Commit to embracing the uncertainty and trusting in the process.

Affirmations for Embracing Change

Here are some affirmations to support you as you embrace change:

1. I trust that change is a natural part of my journey.
2. I am open to the opportunities that change brings into my life.
3. I observe my emotions around change without judgment or fear.
4. I trust myself to navigate change with grace and courage.
5. I embrace the unknown, knowing that it leads to growth and transformation.

Chapter 12

The Art of Letting Go—Releasing What No Longer Serves You

Introduction: Why Letting Go Is So Hard

Letting go is one of the hardest things we're asked to do in life. Whether it's releasing a toxic relationship, an old belief system, a job that no longer fits, or even a past version of ourselves, the act of letting go can feel like an emotional free fall. For many of us, letting go feels like loss, and loss can be terrifying. We hold on because what's familiar, even if it's painful or limiting, feels safer than the unknown.

But there's a beauty in letting go that we often overlook. When we release what no longer serves us, we create space—space for growth, for new opportunities, for healing. Letting go isn't about abandoning what's important; it's about shedding the layers, attachments, and beliefs that are keeping us from fully experiencing life as our authentic selves. It's about trusting that something better awaits on the other side of the release.

Letting go doesn't mean dismissing or forgetting the importance of what you are releasing. Instead, it's about honoring what has played a role in your life and recognizing when it's time to move forward. This chapter will take you through the deeply emotional and empowering process of letting go, guiding you to understand why we hold on and how the HOME Method can help you embrace this process with self-compassion and grace.

Why We Hold On

Before we dive into how to let go, it's important to understand why we hold on in the first place.

We tend to cling to things, people, or ideas because they offer us a sense of stability, even if they're causing us pain. This clinging often stems from fear—the fear of the unknown, the fear of loss, the fear of change.

Our brains are wired to seek familiarity. When we've invested time and energy into something, even if it's not good for us, we become emotionally attached to it. This is why leaving a toxic relationship or a draining job can feel so hard—it's not just about the situation itself but about the emotional investment we've made in it.

Sometimes, we hold onto things because they reinforce the stories we've told ourselves. If you've always believed you're not good enough, you might hold onto relationships or situations that confirm that belief. Letting go would mean challenging that story, and that can feel unsettling.

Story: Holding On to Old Identities

For years, I held onto an identity that was no longer serving me. I believed that in order to be loved, I had to be perfect—always accommodating, always agreeable, never making mistakes. This perfectionism became a part of how I defined myself, and I held onto it even though it was exhausting and damaging.

The idea of letting go of this identity terrified me because it meant stepping into the unknown. Who would I be if I wasn't perfect? Would people still love me if I made mistakes or said no? It wasn't until I realized how much this perfectionism was limiting my life that I began to slowly let go of the need to be everything for everyone.

Letting go of that old identity was a process, not a one-time decision. And even now, I still find myself slipping into old patterns. But with each step, I create more space for authenticity, self-compassion, and a real connection with the people around me.

Why Letting Go Can Feel Like Loss

One of the reasons letting go feels so difficult is because it often feels like a loss. When we let go of something—a relationship, a belief, or even a role we've played for years—it can feel like a part of us is disappearing. We grieve what we're releasing, and it's important to honor that process. Grief isn't just about death; it's also about mourning the end of a chapter or a version of yourself that no longer fits.

The fear of losing something or someone is deeply rooted in our need for connection and stability. Even when the thing we're holding onto is unhealthy or limiting, it can still provide a sense of security. Letting go feels like stepping into the unknown, and that uncertainty can trigger anxiety or fear.

The Healing Power of Letting Go

The first step in letting go is recognizing that holding on to what no longer serves you is preventing you from healing. Whether it's an old belief system, a toxic relationship, or a painful memory, clinging to it keeps you stuck in patterns that are hindering your growth.

Letting go isn't about forgetting or dismissing the importance of what you're releasing—it's about honoring the role it has played in your life and recognizing when it's time to move forward. When you let go, you make space for new experiences, relationships, and healing. The act of letting go is, in itself, a form of healing.

Story: Letting Go After Loss

When I lost my sister, the grief felt unbearable. For a long time, I clung to the pain, believing that if I let go of it, I would somehow be letting go of her. I thought that holding onto my sadness was the only way to keep her memory alive. But over time, I realized that the grief was preventing me from fully living my own life.

Letting go of the constant sorrow didn't mean I was forgetting her—it meant I was allowing myself to heal. By releasing the grip that pain had on me, I made room for joy, love, and new memories. I still carry my sister's memory with me every day, but I've learned to let go of the idea that healing means losing her. Healing meant finding a new way to honor her while also allowing myself to live.

Step 1: Healing—Recognizing What Needs to Be Released

The first step in letting go is Healing. This begins with recognizing what you need to release and why. What is no longer serving you? What is holding you back from growth or peace?

Sometimes, what needs to be let go of is obvious—a toxic relationship, a job that's making you miserable. But other times, it's more subtle. It could be a belief system that's been ingrained in you since childhood or an emotional attachment to an old identity.

Once you've identified what needs to be released, it's important to acknowledge the role it has played in your life. Even the things that harm us often serve a purpose. They might protect us from vulnerability or confirm an old belief we're afraid to challenge. But once you recognize that holding on is causing more harm than good, you can begin the process of healing.

Example: I spent years holding onto the belief that I had to take care of everyone around me.

This belief served me for a long time—it made me feel needed and valued, and it protected me from the fear of being abandoned. But over time, it became clear that this belief was also causing me deep exhaustion and resentment. Recognizing that I needed to let go of this old belief was the first step toward healing and reclaiming my own needs.

Letting go of this belief didn't happen overnight. I had to sit with the discomfort of setting boundaries, feeling guilty for prioritizing myself, and facing my fear of being seen as selfish. But each time I chose to release the need to care for everyone else, I experienced a small healing. The more I let go, the more I was able to heal the wounds that had kept me stuck.

Step 2: Observing—Witnessing Your Attachments Without Judgment

The second step in letting go is Observing. Once you've identified what needs to be released, the next step is to observe your attachment to it. This requires you to become a witness to your thoughts and emotions without judgment. Why are you holding on? What fear or need is keeping you attached to this person, belief, or situation?

By observing your attachment without judgment, you create space between you and the thing you're holding onto. You start to see it for what it really is rather than what you've built it up to be in your mind. This clarity helps you loosen your grip and opens the door to release.

Example: I once held onto a friendship that was no longer healthy. Every interaction left me feeling drained, but I couldn't bring myself to let go. When I started observing my attachment to this friendship, I realized that I was holding on out of fear—fear of being alone, fear of losing the history we had shared. Once I saw that this fear was at the root of my attachment, I was able to let go with more compassion for myself and the relationship.

Observing my attachment allowed me to see the dynamics of the friendship more clearly. I noticed how much energy I was putting into maintaining the relationship and how little I was receiving in return. I also saw how holding onto this friendship was preventing me from opening up to new, healthier connections. By observing without judgment, I was able to release the friendship with gratitude for what it had taught me and with the understanding that it was time to move on.

Step 3: Mindfulness—Letting Go With Presence

Mindfulness plays a crucial role in the process of letting go. When we hold on to something—whether it's a memory, a belief, or a relationship—we often do so unconsciously. The act of clinging becomes a habit, something we do without even realizing it. By practicing Mindfulness, we bring awareness to our attachment, allowing us to make a conscious choice to release it.

Letting go with mindfulness means staying present in the moment, even when it's uncomfortable. It means being with the emotions that arise when you think about letting go and allowing yourself to feel the fear, sadness, or relief that comes with it.

Story: Practicing Mindfulness as My Daughter Graduated from High School

One of the hardest things for me to let go of was the phase of my life where I was an active, hands-on mother. When my daughter graduated from high school, I had an incredibly difficult time accepting that she was now an adult. I found myself grieving the idea that I would no longer drive her to school, attend parent-teacher conferences, or play that same day-to-day role in her life.

As the graduation day approached, I felt a deep sense of loss. I kept replaying memories of her childhood, and I struggled with the fact that those days were over. But instead of letting the sadness take over, I decided to practice mindfulness. I sat with the emotions, acknowledging how bittersweet they were. I allowed myself to feel both the sadness of letting go of her childhood and the pride I had in the woman she had become.

Through mindfulness, I shifted my perspective. Instead of focusing on what I was losing, I started celebrating what I had gained. I raised an amazing, intelligent, and capable daughter. And in that moment, I realized that the end of one chapter meant the beginning of a new one. I congratulated myself for raising her and for allowing myself to move forward into this next phase with gratitude and pride. Letting go of her childhood didn't mean losing her—it meant welcoming a new, even more rewarding relationship with her as an adult.

Step 4: Embracing—Welcoming What Comes After the Release

The final step is Embracing. Letting go is an act of trust. It requires you to believe that by releasing what no longer serves you, you are creating space for something better. Embracing means welcoming whatever comes after the release—whether it's a sense of peace, a new opportunity, or a deeper connection to yourself.

Embracing doesn't mean that letting go is easy or painless. It means that you are willing to move through the discomfort and trust that on the other side, there is growth, healing, and possibility.

Example: After letting go of the belief that I had to be perfect, I was left with a lot of uncertainty. I didn't know who I was without that identity. But over time, I began to embrace the freedom that came with it. I allowed myself to make mistakes, to set boundaries, and to be more honest about my needs. In doing so, I found a deeper sense of self-acceptance and connection to others.

Embracing also means recognizing that letting go often opens the door to unexpected blessings. Whether it's a new friendship, a renewed sense of purpose, or simply the relief of no longer carrying the burden of something that no longer fits, embracing the aftermath of release allows you to step into new opportunities with open arms.

Exercise: Practicing the Art of Letting Go with the HOME Method

Here's an exercise to help you practice letting go using the HOME Method:

1. **Healing:** Identify something in your life that you need to let go of. This could be a relationship, a belief, or an old identity. Reflect on how holding onto it has been preventing your healing.

2. **Observing:** Observe your attachment to this person, belief, or situation without judgment. What fear or need is keeping you from letting go? What emotions arise when you think about releasing it?

3. **Mindfulness:** Practice being present with the emotions that come up when you think about letting go. Stay with the discomfort, sadness, or fear without pushing it away. Use your breath to anchor yourself in the present moment.

4. **Embracing:** Once you've worked through the emotions, reflect on what comes next. What new opportunities or experiences might arise once you've let go? How can you embrace the space you've created by releasing what no longer serves you?

Affirmations for Letting Go

Here are some affirmations to help you in the process of letting go:

1. I trust that letting go will create space for growth and healing.
2. I release what no longer serves me with compassion and grace.
3. I allow myself to feel the emotions that come with letting go.
4. I embrace the possibilities that come with change and release.
5. I trust that I am supported in my journey of letting go and healing.

Chapter 13

Trusting the Process—Learning to Surrender Control

Introduction: The Illusion of Control

As human beings, we love control. We crave certainty, structure, and predictability in our lives. Control gives us a sense of safety, a feeling that we can manage outcomes and avoid unpleasant surprises. But life rarely operates according to our plans, and the reality is that much of what happens around us is beyond our control. Trying to grasp onto every situation, every relationship, and every outcome only creates frustration, anxiety, and stress.

Surrendering control can feel incredibly vulnerable, but it is also one of the most freeing and necessary parts of the healing journey. Letting go of the need to micromanage every detail of life doesn't mean giving up or being passive—it means trusting the process. It's about having faith in the flow of life, in your ability to navigate challenges, and in the unseen forces that guide you.

This chapter is about learning to release the tight grip of control and surrendering to the journey, even when you can't see the destination.

Why We Try to Control Everything

Control is often rooted in fear—fear of the unknown, fear of failure, fear of disappointment, or fear of loss. When we feel vulnerable or unsure of what the future holds, we naturally want to impose structure on the situation. We want to know what will happen, when it will happen, and how it will turn out. This desire for control can show up in many ways—rigid planning, overthinking, trying to "fix" people or situations, or avoiding anything that feels unpredictable.

Control gives us the illusion that we can protect ourselves from pain or discomfort. If we can just plan everything perfectly, then maybe we can avoid the heartbreak, the disappointment, or the uncertainty. But the truth is, life doesn't always follow our plans. Unexpected events, detours, and challenges are inevitable, and the harder we try to control everything, the more resistance and frustration we create.

Story: My Struggle with Control

For many years, I tried to control every aspect of my life. I believed that if I planned everything carefully, I could avoid failure or disappointment. This need for control showed up in my work, my relationships, and even in how I approached my emotions. I would make detailed plans for how my life "should" unfold and would become deeply frustrated and anxious when things didn't go as expected.

In my personal relationships, I often tried to control how others behaved or responded. If a partner didn't act in a way that I had anticipated or wanted, I would feel hurt and angry, convinced that if I could just do something differently, I could "fix" the situation. Over time, this need for control started to create tension, both within myself and with the people around me.

It wasn't until I started practicing surrender—letting go of the need to micromanage every detail—that I began to experience true freedom. Surrendering didn't mean I stopped caring about my life or my relationships. It meant that I stopped trying to force everything to fit into a perfect box. I learned to trust that even when things didn't go according to plan, there was still value in the experience.

The Power of Surrender

Surrender is not the same as giving up. Surrender is about releasing the need to control outcomes and trusting that, even if things don't go the way you planned, they will unfold as they need to.

It's about recognizing that there are forces at work beyond our comprehension and that trying to control every detail only creates resistance.

Surrendering allows you to flow with life rather than fight against it. It teaches you to let go of rigid expectations and embrace the present moment as it is without needing it to be different. Surrendering control opens up the possibility for unexpected opportunities, deeper connections, and more joy because you're no longer trying to force life into a narrow box.

Story: Learning to Surrender After Moving to a New Country

One of the most profound experiences where I learned to surrender was when I moved to a new country in my early twenties. It was one of the most difficult and uncertain times of my life.

After the tragic loss of my sister, I was searching for healing, but I had no idea where to find it.

Deep in grief and feeling lost, I instinctively knew I needed a change, something that would force me out of my comfort zone and into a place where I could rebuild.

Moving to a foreign country where I knew no one and had never been before was an enormous leap of faith. I had no idea how things would turn out. The uncertainty was terrifying, but I felt that staying where I was—emotionally, mentally, and physically—would hold me back from healing. I had a vision of what I wanted, but there was so much that I couldn't control.

At first, I tried to micromanage the experience. I wanted to know every detail about the place I was moving to, plan out how my life would unfold, and make sure that everything went "right."

But life had other plans, and soon, I realized that no matter how much I tried to control the situation, things wouldn't always turn out as I expected.

Slowly, I began to surrender to the process. I let go of the need to control every outcome and allowed myself to experience the highs and lows of this massive change. In the process, I discovered an inner strength I didn't know I had. What I thought was going to be a terrifying leap turned into one of the most rewarding experiences of my life. Letting go of control opened the door to opportunities, new friendships, and growth I could never have planned for.

Through this experience, I learned that surrendering wasn't about giving up on my dreams or desires—it was about trusting that life would take me where I needed to go, even if I couldn't see the path clearly. By releasing control, I allowed space for something even better than what I had originally imagined.

Step 1: Healing—Releasing Control as a Healing Practice

The first step in surrendering control is recognizing that holding onto it can be a barrier to healing. When we try to control every aspect of our lives, we leave little room for growth, spontaneity, or the possibility of transformation. Control often keeps us stuck in old patterns because it's tied to our desire for safety and predictability.

To heal, we must release the need to know and control every outcome. This doesn't mean abandoning responsibility—it means trusting that things will unfold in their own time and in their own way and that the process itself is part of the healing journey. Releasing control invites more flow into your life, allowing you to heal from the rigidity of perfectionism, fear, or the need to "fix" everything.

Example: I realized that my need for control in my personal relationships stemmed from old wounds around abandonment. I thought that if I could control how people behaved or felt, I could avoid being hurt. But this constant need to control drained me and prevented real intimacy. By recognizing that my desire for control was a response to fear, I was able to start healing that wound and release the need to control every situation.

Step 2: Observing—Noticing Your Patterns of Control

The second step is Observing. Once you've recognized that control is preventing you from healing or moving forward, the next step is to observe when and where you try to control things in your life. This requires awareness and self-reflection. Are there specific areas of your life where you feel a constant need to manage outcomes? Do you try to control how others behave or how situations unfold?

By observing these patterns without judgment, you begin to see where you might be holding on too tightly. You can start to notice how this need for control affects your emotional state, your relationships, and your overall sense of well-being. Often, control is linked to anxiety, fear, or a deep-seated desire for certainty. By observing your need for control, you can bring awareness to the underlying emotions driving it.

Do You See This in Your Life?

Take a moment to reflect on your relationships, both personal and professional. Do you notice a pattern of wanting to control situations? For example, are you constantly trying to manage the dynamics between you and your significant other? Do you try to "fix" how they approach problems, hoping they'll handle things the way you would? Or maybe you've experienced this at work—feeling the urge to control how projects unfold or needing to dictate how your team or your boss approaches decisions.

Control in relationships often shows up as a desire to change or manage the behavior of others. It can be subtle, like making suggestions that are really disguised as demands, or it can be more obvious, like wanting your partner to follow a strict plan or routine. The same applies in professional settings—perhaps you feel anxious when colleagues don't handle tasks the way you would, or you overthink every detail of a project, fearing that if something slips through the cracks, it will reflect poorly on you.

By simply observing these patterns, you'll start to see where control might be creeping in and how it impacts your life. The key here is not to judge yourself but to become aware of where control shows up and what emotions or fears are driving it.

Step 3: Mindfulness—Practicing Presence and Letting Go

Once you've observed your patterns of control, the next step is to practice Mindfulness. Mindfulness invites you to stay present in the moment, even when things feel chaotic or uncertain. When you practice mindfulness, you're training your mind to focus on what's happening right now rather than worrying about what might happen in the future or trying to control the outcome.

Practicing mindfulness doesn't mean ignoring your desire for control—it means noticing when that desire arises and choosing to stay present instead. It's about trusting that the present moment holds exactly what you need, even if it doesn't look the way you expected.

Story: Mindfulness in Parenting

One of the most challenging moments in my life was learning to let go of control as a parent. When my daughter graduated from high school, I struggled deeply with the idea that she was now an adult. I wanted to keep guiding her to make sure she was safe and on the "right" path.

But I knew that this phase of parenting required me to let go. She needed the space to make her own choices, even if they didn't align with my vision for her future.

Through mindfulness, I was able to stay present during this transition. I focused on celebrating her achievements rather than trying to control what came next. I trusted that the values I had instilled in her were strong enough to guide her, and I allowed myself to release the need to manage every detail of her life.

Step 4: Embracing—Trusting the Unknown

The final step in surrendering control is Embracing. This means embracing the uncertainty of life and trusting that even when you don't know the outcome, things will unfold in the way they are meant to. Embracing the unknown requires a deep level of trust—not just in the universe but in yourself. It means trusting that you are capable of handling whatever comes your way, even if it doesn't align with your original plans.

Embracing the unknown doesn't mean abandoning your goals or desires—it means allowing them to unfold naturally without forcing or controlling every aspect. It means believing that what is meant for you will not pass you by and that sometimes, the best things in life come when we let go of the need to control every outcome.

Affirmations for Letting Go and Trusting the Process

Here are some affirmations to help you release control and surrender to the process of life with trust and confidence:

1. I trust that everything is unfolding exactly as it should, even when I cannot see the outcome.

2.   I release the need to control others and allow them the freedom to be themselves.

3.   I embrace uncertainty, knowing that it brings new possibilities and growth into my life.

4.   I let go of the fear of the unknown and trust in the journey ahead.

5.   I am open to the flow of life and release the need to micromanage every detail.

6.   I am confident in my ability to handle whatever comes my way, even when things don't go as planned.

7.   I trust that what is meant for me will not pass me by.

8.   I release old patterns of control and invite peace and acceptance into my life.

9.   I allow myself to be present in this moment, knowing that the present holds everything I need.

10.   I embrace the process of life and surrender to the unknown with faith and grace.

11.   I am free to flow with life's changes, trusting that each shift brings me closer to my authentic self.

12.   I honor my journey and trust that each step I take is leading me toward healing and growth.

13.   I release my grip on the need for control and trust the wisdom of life's natural unfolding.

14.   I accept that I cannot control every outcome, and I allow life to guide me to new opportunities.

Chapter 14

Finding Balance Between Surrender and Action— When to Let Go and When to Take Charge

Introduction: The Dance Between Surrender and Action

One of the great challenges in life is learning to find the balance between surrender and action. We often hear advice to "let go and trust the process," but at the same time, we know there are moments when we must step up, take charge, and take decisive action in our lives. How do we know when to surrender and let go and when to assert ourselves and create change?

Life is a constant dance between these two forces—allowing and acting. Too much control can cause resistance, but too much surrender without action can leave us feeling powerless or stuck. In this chapter, we'll explore how to find harmony between these two powerful forces, using the HOME Method to help you navigate when it's time to release and when it's time to take action.

Why We Get Stuck in One Mode

Before we dive into finding the balance, it's important to understand why we often get stuck in either a state of too much action or too much surrender. These imbalances usually come from fear, past experiences, or deeply ingrained beliefs about ourselves and the world.

- **Overaction and Control:** For many of us, there's a strong impulse to control our lives through constant action. We believe that by "doing" more, we can fix situations, avoid discomfort, or ensure the outcome we desire. This often comes from a place of fear—fear of the unknown, fear of failure, or fear of loss. As a result, we may over-plan, overwork, or push others in an effort to control outcomes.

- **Over-Surrendering and Passivity:** On the other hand, some of us fall into the trap of too much surrender. We may believe that life happens to us rather than understanding that we have the power to create change. In this state, we may avoid taking responsibility or action because we're afraid of making the wrong choice or because we've internalized a belief that we're powerless. Over-surrendering can lead to feelings of helplessness or stagnation.

The key is to find balance—knowing when to trust the flow of life and when to assert your power to create the changes you desire.

Understanding the Balance: Surrender and Action as Complementary Forces

Surrender and action are not opposing forces but rather complementary ones. Just as a river flows naturally but still carves its path through the landscape, we, too, must learn when to flow with life and when to direct our energy toward shaping it.

Think of surrender as your ability to trust life's natural flow, release control and allow things to unfold organically. Action, on the other hand, is your ability to make decisions, set boundaries, and pursue goals with intention. Both are needed to live a balanced, fulfilling life.

When you lean too far into surrender without taking any action, you risk feeling passive, stagnant, or at the mercy of life's circumstances. Conversely, when you overemphasize action and try to control everything, you may feel anxious, frustrated, and burned out. The sweet spot lies in knowing when to let go and when to act.

Step 1: Healing—Releasing the Fear of "Getting It Wrong"

The first step in finding balance is Healing—specifically, releasing the fear that you'll "get it wrong." Much of our struggle with the balance between surrender and action comes from the fear of making mistakes. We worry that if we don't control everything, things will fall apart. At the same time, we fear that if we act too soon or make the wrong choice, we'll ruin our chances of happiness or success.

To find peace in this dance, we must heal the belief that there is only one right way to do things. There is no "perfect" moment to act, and there is no "perfect" path. Healing means accepting that life is filled with trial and error and that both surrender and action are necessary steps along the way. Trust that the mistakes you make will teach you valuable lessons and that sometimes, inaction is just as instructive.

Story: My Fear of Overacting in Relationships

I used to struggle with the belief that I always needed to be in control of my relationships. I was afraid that if I didn't constantly "manage" things—if I didn't control the dynamic—I'd lose the relationship or be abandoned. As a result, I often overacted. I would push too hard, try to fix problems immediately or take on the emotional weight of the relationship, believing it was my responsibility to hold everything together.

But as I began to heal, I realized that my constant overaction was coming from a place of fear, not love. I wasn't trusting the natural flow of the relationship or giving my partner the space to be themselves. Once I began to release this fear and trust more, I learned that sometimes, stepping back and letting things unfold was the healthiest choice. My relationship became stronger when I allowed more room for balance.

Step 2: Observing—Identifying Your Patterns

The next step is Observing your patterns. Do you tend to overact, pushing yourself and others to make things happen? Or do you often fall into passivity, waiting for life to change without taking any action? Begin by identifying your tendencies in various areas of your life—relationships, career, personal growth.

Consider these questions:

- Are there times when I try to control everything, making plans or decisions out of fear?
- Do I often hesitate or avoid taking action because I'm afraid of making the wrong choice?
- In my relationships, do I tend to be the one who takes charge, or do I often wait for the other person to take the lead?

As you observe these patterns, remember that neither extreme is inherently "wrong." The goal is not to label yourself but to gain awareness of how you navigate the balance between surrender and action.

Do You See This in Your Life?

Think about your relationships. Are there times when you find yourself trying to control the dynamics with your partner? Perhaps you're the one always planning the next step, trying to resolve conflicts immediately, or guiding the course of the relationship. Or, on the other hand, maybe you find yourself waiting for your partner to make decisions, hoping that things will "just work out" without you having to step in.

You might also notice this in your work life. Are you someone who often takes on too much, believing that if you don't control every detail, the project will fail? Or do you avoid taking the lead, hoping that someone else will make the tough decisions?

By simply observing these patterns, you can begin to understand where you might need more balance between surrender and action.

Step 3: Mindfulness—Pausing to Find Clarity

After observing your patterns, the next step is to practice Mindfulness. When you notice yourself slipping into either overaction or over-surrender, pause. Take a moment to ground yourself in the present and ask: What does this moment require?

Mindfulness allows you to tune into your inner wisdom and the energy of the situation. Sometimes, the answer will be clear—it's time to act, to set boundaries, or to take charge of a situation. Other times, the answer will be to trust the flow and allow things to unfold naturally.

Practicing mindfulness in this way will help you develop the discernment needed to know when to surrender and when to take action.

Example: Finding Balance in Parenting

As a parent, I often found myself struggling with when to step in and when to step back. There were times when my instinct was to jump in and control the situation, thinking that if I didn't intervene, things would go wrong. But as my children grew older, I realized that they needed the space to figure things out for themselves.

Through mindfulness, I learned to pause before reacting. When my daughter was going through challenges in school, I felt the urge to step in and solve the problem. But by pausing, I was able to ask myself: Is this a time for action or a time to trust that she can handle it? Often, the answer was to step back, let her navigate the situation, and trust that she would grow from the experience.

Step 4: Embracing—Leaning Into Both Surrender and Action

The final step is Embracing the balance between surrender and action. Life is constantly asking us to find harmony between these two forces. By embracing both, you allow yourself to flow with the rhythm of life—taking action when necessary and trusting the process when it's time to let go.

Embrace the times when you need to take action. Set your intentions, pursue your goals, and make decisions with confidence. But also embrace the moments when you need to let go, trust the process, and allow things to unfold in their own time.

Story: Embracing the Balance in My Career

There was a time in my career when I was torn between taking bold action and waiting for the right opportunity to present itself. I had an idea for a new project, but I wasn't sure whether to pursue it or wait for a sign that it was the right time.

After practicing mindfulness, I realized that I needed both—action and surrender. I took the first steps by outlining my vision and putting in the initial work, but then I had to surrender to the timing of the universe. I couldn't control every detail or outcome, and I needed to trust that the right opportunities would come in their own time.

By embracing this balance, I found that things began to align naturally. I was able to pursue my goals with passion while also remaining open to the unexpected opportunities that came my way.

Tools for Discerning Between Surrender and Action

Finding the balance between surrender and action requires self-awareness and the ability to listen to your inner wisdom. Here are some tools and leading questions to help you discern when it's time to take action and when it's time to let go:

1. **Reflect on Your Energy Levels**

   - Ask yourself: Am I feeling energized and ready to take steps, or am I feeling drained and overwhelmed?

   - If you're feeling motivated and energized, it might be a sign that it's time to take action. If you're feeling exhausted, it might be time to surrender and allow things to flow.

2. **Check Your Emotional State**

   - Ask yourself: Am I making decisions from a place of fear or from a place of calm clarity?

   - If you notice that your urge to act comes from anxiety or fear of losing control, pause. Take a step back and consider whether it's time to surrender instead. Action taken from a place of calm clarity tends to be more effective and aligned with your true intentions.

3. **Tune into the Situation**

   - Ask yourself: Is this situation something I can directly influence, or is it beyond my control?

   - Sometimes, we try to act on things that are simply out of our hands—such as other people's behavior or external circumstances. Recognizing when a situation is beyond your control is key to knowing when to surrender.

4. **Consider Timing**

   - Ask yourself: Is now the right time to act, or would it be better to wait and gather more information?

- Timing is crucial when balancing surrender and action. Sometimes, waiting allows more clarity to emerge. Other times, hesitation can lead to missed opportunities. Trust your intuition on whether the timing feels right.

5. **Ask for Signs or Guidance**

- Ask yourself: Am I receiving any signs or nudges that it's time to move forward?

- Often, life provides subtle signs or opportunities when it's time to act. Pay attention to synchronicities or repeated messages that might be guiding you toward taking a step.

Exercise: Finding Balance Between Surrender and Action

Here's an exercise to help you practice balancing surrender and action using the HOME Method:

1. **Healing:** Reflect on areas of your life where you may be acting out of fear or over-control. What old wounds or fears are driving this need for control? Write down one belief you can begin to heal.

2. **Observing:** Notice your patterns. In what situations do you tend to overact, trying to control every outcome? Where do you tend to surrender too much, avoiding action or responsibility?

3. **Mindfulness:** Next time you feel the urge to control a situation or, conversely, the temptation to avoid taking action, pause. Ask yourself: What does this moment require? Allow your inner wisdom to guide you.

4.   **Embracing:** Choose one situation where you will practice both surrender and action. Take a small step toward your goal, and then trust that the rest will unfold naturally. Embrace both your ability to act and your ability to let go.

Affirmations for Finding Balance Between Surrender and Action

Here are some affirmations to help you find balance:

1.   I trust myself to know when to act and when to let go.
2.   I release the need to control every outcome and embrace the flow of life.
3.   I take action with intention while trusting that the universe will guide me.
4.   I am capable of making decisions and creating change in my life.
5.   I trust that what is meant for me will come in its own time.
6.   I embrace the balance between taking charge and surrendering control.
7.   I am open to both action and stillness, knowing that each has its place in my journey.
8.   I trust that I can handle whatever life brings, even when I don't have all the answers.
9.   I allow myself to flow between surrender and action with grace and confidence.
10.   I am grounded in the present, knowing that each step I take brings me closer to balance.

Chapter 15

Cultivating Patience—Trusting in Divine Timing

Introduction: The Challenge of Patience

In a world that constantly pushes for instant gratification, cultivating patience can feel like a forgotten art. We want quick answers, immediate results, and fast fixes for the problems we face. Waiting, however, can stir up feelings of frustration, doubt, and even fear. When things aren't moving as quickly as we'd like, it's easy to question whether our desires will ever manifest or if we're on the right path at all.

But patience is a crucial part of personal growth, healing, and the spiritual journey. It's the ability to trust that everything is unfolding in perfect timing, even when we can't see the full picture.

Divine timing doesn't always align with our own expectations or desires, but it often brings something better than we could have planned ourselves. In this chapter, we'll explore the importance of patience—especially the importance of being patient with yourself—and how the HOME Method can help you develop trust in the timing of your life.

Why Patience Is So Difficult

Patience is challenging because it asks us to let go of control, certainty, and often our attachment to specific outcomes. When we are in a state of waiting—whether for a relationship, a career opportunity, or healing—it can feel like we're stuck in limbo. This discomfort arises from not knowing when, or even if, things will turn out the way we hope.

Our culture reinforces the idea that faster is better. We see people achieving success, love, and personal goals seemingly overnight, and we begin to compare ourselves, wondering why we're not there yet. This comparison often extends to how we feel about ourselves, leading to impatience with our own journey. We question why we aren't healing faster, growing quicker, or reaching our goals as soon as we think we should. But what if we shifted our perspective on waiting and patience—not just with life's circumstances but with ourselves?

Being Patient with Yourself: A Key Part of Growth

One of the most important aspects of patience is being patient with yourself. Personal growth, healing, and transformation are not linear processes, and yet, we often expect ourselves to grow at a rapid, predictable pace. When progress feels slow, we may become frustrated or judgmental toward ourselves, believing that we're not doing enough or that we should be further along by now.

Learning to be patient with yourself means accepting that growth takes time and that healing doesn't happen overnight. It's about allowing yourself the space to make mistakes, take detours, and move at your own pace without self-criticism. When you cultivate self-patience, you stop measuring your progress against unrealistic timelines or comparing your journey to others.

Story: Learning to Be Patient with My Healing Process

For many years, I was impatient with my own healing process. After experiencing deep trauma and grief, I wanted to move through the pain as quickly as possible. I believed that if I worked hard enough, I could speed up my recovery. But healing doesn't follow a schedule, and the more I pushed, the more frustrated I became when I didn't feel "better" right away.

It wasn't until I began practicing patience with myself that I realized healing isn't something I can rush. I learned to be gentler with myself, to honor the days when I didn't feel strong or productive, and to accept that some wounds take time to heal. By releasing the pressure to "heal faster," I created space for real growth and self-compassion.

Understanding Divine Timing

Divine timing is the belief that everything happens when it's supposed to, not necessarily when we want it to. It's the idea that life is guided by a force greater than ourselves—whether you call it the universe, God, or your higher self—and that this force has a wisdom we may not always understand in the moment.

When we trust in divine timing, we let go of the pressure to force things into being. We release the need for immediate gratification and accept that things are unfolding exactly as they should. This doesn't mean that we passively wait for life to happen, but rather that we align ourselves with the flow of life and trust that the right opportunities, relationships, and experiences will come when the time is right.

Story: Learning to Trust Divine Timing After a Major Life Change

One of the most significant lessons in patience for me came after a major move to another country. As I shared earlier, it was a leap of faith—one I took when I was in deep grief and searching for healing. But even after I made the move, I didn't find the peace and clarity I expected right away. In fact, it took years before I felt truly settled, emotionally and spiritually.

During those years, I questioned whether I had made the right decision. I was impatient for healing, impatient for a clear direction, and frustrated that my life wasn't unfolding the way I had envisioned. But with time, I began to realize that this period of uncertainty was part of my growth. Divine timing was at work. The experiences I had during that time—the challenges, the waiting, the introspection—were preparing me for the next phase of my life. It wasn't until I surrendered to the timing of my healing that I found peace and began to see the gifts that came from the waiting period.

Step 1: Healing—Releasing the Need for Immediate Answers

The first step in cultivating patience is Healing the need for immediate answers. Many of us struggle with waiting because we fear that if we don't have the answers now, we'll lose control or miss out on something important. This fear drives us to rush decisions or force outcomes, which can lead to choices we later regret.

To heal this fear, we need to release the belief that everything needs to happen on our timeline. This doesn't mean giving up on your goals or desires, but it does mean allowing space for the unknown and trusting that clarity will come in its own time.

Story: Releasing My Need for Immediate Success

There was a point in my life when I was obsessed with achieving success on a specific timeline. I had a vision of where I wanted my career to go, and I pushed myself relentlessly to make it happen. But the more I forced things, the more obstacles seemed to appear. It was as if the universe was telling me to slow down, but I wasn't listening.

Eventually, I burned out. I was frustrated, exhausted, and questioning whether I was even on the right path. It wasn't until I took a step back and released my need for immediate success that things began to shift. By healing my attachment to a specific timeline, I allowed space for opportunities to come in their own time. Slowly, things began to fall into place, and I realized that my need for immediate answers had been blocking me from receiving what was truly aligned with my path.

Step 2: Observing—Recognizing Where Impatience Shows Up

The next step is Observing where impatience shows up in your life. Often, impatience is a sign that we're uncomfortable with uncertainty. We may feel anxious, frustrated, or even angry when things don't move as quickly as we want them to.

Start by identifying the areas of your life where you feel the most impatient. Is it in your relationships where you're waiting for a partner or a deeper connection? Is it in your career where you're eager for promotion or recognition? Or perhaps it's in your personal growth where you feel like you should be "further along" by now.

By observing where impatience arises, you can begin to see the underlying fears or beliefs driving it.

Do You See This in Your Life?

- Are you constantly checking your phone, hoping for a message or update that will change your situation?

- Do you find yourself rushing through tasks or projects, eager to get to the next thing, without fully appreciating where you are now?

- In your relationships, do you feel frustrated when progress isn't happening as quickly as you'd like, whether it's waiting for commitment, healing, or a resolution?

- Are you hard on yourself when your personal growth feels slow or when you're not where you think you should be?

Impatience often shows up as a desire to fast-forward through the uncomfortable or uncertain parts of life. By observing these tendencies without judgment, you can begin to create space for patience—not only with life but with yourself.

Step 3: Mindfulness—Staying Present While You Wait

Once you've observed where impatience shows up, the next step is Mindfulness. Practicing mindfulness allows you to stay present in the moment, even when things aren't moving as quickly as you'd like. When we focus too much on the future—on when something will happen or how long it will take—we miss the opportunities, lessons, and beauty of the present.

Mindfulness is about accepting where you are right now without rushing to the next step. It's about trusting that everything you need in this moment is already here, even if it's not what you expected. By grounding yourself in the present, you can release the tension that comes from waiting and allow life to unfold naturally.

Story: Mindfulness During a Challenging Time

After moving to a new country, I spent a long time feeling out of place. I was impatient for the clarity and healing that I thought would come right away. But the more I focused on what wasn't happening, the more frustrated I became.

It wasn't until I started practicing mindfulness—focusing on the present moment instead of the future—that I began to feel more at peace. I started to appreciate the small moments of joy and growth that were happening in my daily life, even if they weren't the big breakthroughs I was hoping for. By staying present, I learned to trust that everything was unfolding in its own time.

Step 4: Embracing—Leaning Into the Timing of Your Life

The final step is Embracing the timing of your life. This means accepting that things may not happen exactly when or how you planned but trusting that they will happen when the time is right. Embracing divine timing is about letting go of the need to control every outcome and instead allowing life to guide you.

When you embrace the timing of your life, you stop fighting against the current and start flowing with it. You trust that even in the waiting, you are exactly where you need to be. You understand that the pauses, delays, and detours are all part of your journey and that they are preparing you for what's to come.

Story: Embracing Divine Timing in Love

There was a period in my life when I was impatient for love. I wanted a deep connection, a soulmate, and I was frustrated that it wasn't happening on my timeline. I questioned whether I was doing something wrong or if love would ever come my way.

But as I worked on myself, healed old wounds, and practiced patience, I realized that the time I spent waiting wasn't wasted. It was a time of preparation. When love finally did come into my life, it was more aligned, more fulfilling, and more genuine than I could have imagined. I realized that if it had come sooner, I wouldn't have been ready to receive it fully. By embracing divine timing, I opened myself up to the love that was meant for me.

Tools for Cultivating Patience with Yourself and Trusting Divine Timing

To help you cultivate patience and trust in divine timing, here are some tools and reflective questions to guide you:

1. **Reframe Waiting as Preparation**
   - Ask yourself: How is this period of waiting to prepare me for what's to come?

- Instead of seeing waiting as a void, view it as a time of growth, reflection, and preparation. Ask yourself what you are learning at this moment and how it's helping you become the person you need to be for the next phase of your life.

2. **Be Gentle with Yourself**

- Ask yourself: Am I being too hard on myself? How can I offer myself more compassion and patience as I navigate this phase?

- It's easy to be your own harshest critic, but remember that growth takes time. Be gentle with yourself as you move through challenges, and remind yourself that progress—no matter how slow—is still progress.

3. **Practice Gratitude for the Present**

- Ask yourself: What can I appreciate about this moment, even if it's not what I expected?

- Gratitude helps shift your focus from what's missing to what's already here. By practicing gratitude for the present, you begin to trust that everything is unfolding as it should.

4. **Release the Timeline**

- Ask yourself: What would it feel like to let go of my need for things to happen on my timeline?

- Sometimes, our impatience comes from an attachment to when we think things should happen. Practice releasing the need for things to occur on a specific timeline and trust that they will come when the time is right.

5. **Look for Signs of Progress**

- Ask yourself: What small signs of progress can I notice, even if the big outcome hasn't arrived yet?

- Often, progress is happening behind the scenes, even if we can't see the full picture. Look for small shifts, changes, or insights that show you that you're moving in the right direction.

Exercise: Cultivating Patience with Yourself and the World Using the HOME Method

Here's an exercise to help you practice patience and trust divine timing using the HOME Method:

1. **Healing:** Reflect on an area of your life where you feel impatient—with yourself or with a situation. What fears or beliefs are driving your impatience? Write down one belief you can begin to heal (e.g., "I believe that if it doesn't happen now, it never will.").

2. **Observing:** Notice where impatience shows up in your life. Is it in your relationships, career, or personal growth? Observe how impatience affects your emotional state and decision-making.

3. **Mindfulness:** Practice staying present the next time you feel impatient. Focus on what you can appreciate about the present

moment, and remind yourself that everything is unfolding as it should.

4. **Embracing:** Choose one situation where you will embrace divine timing. Let go of the need to control the outcome or timeline and trust that the right opportunity, relationship, or experience will come when it's meant to.

Affirmations for Cultivating Patience with Yourself and Trusting Divine Timing

Here are some affirmations to help you develop patience and trust in divine timing:

1. I trust that everything is unfolding in perfect timing.
2. I release the need for immediate answers and allow space for clarity to come.
3. I embrace the waiting period, knowing it is preparing me for what's next.
4. I trust that what is meant for me will come in its own time.
5. I release my attachment to specific timelines and trust the flow of life.
6. I am exactly where I need to be at this moment.
7. I trust that I am growing and healing at my own pace.
8. I am patient with myself as I move through challenges and growth.
9. I trust the universe's timing and know that everything is working in my favor.
10. I release impatience and embrace the present moment with gratitude.

Chapter 16

Self-Love as the Foundation of Healing—Nurturing Yourself Along the Way

Introduction: The Power of Self-Love

Self-love is a concept we hear about often, but what does it truly mean to love yourself? More importantly, how does self-love shape your healing journey? In this chapter, we'll explore self-love as the foundation of all growth, transformation, and healing. Without self-love, it becomes difficult to move forward because we're constantly undermining ourselves with criticism, shame, or feelings of unworthiness.

Many of us think of self-love as something superficial—treating ourselves to nice things or indulging in occasional self-care. While these acts are important, true self-love runs much deeper. It's about accepting yourself fully, forgiving your past mistakes, and committing to your own well-being. Self-love is the foundation upon which all healing is built. If you're able to cultivate deep compassion, kindness, and respect for yourself, everything else in your life begins to shift.

But self-love isn't always easy, especially when we've been conditioned to believe that we're not enough. Many of us carry wounds from childhood, relationships, or societal pressures that make it hard to feel worthy of love and care. This chapter is about rediscovering and nurturing that love for yourself, understanding its vital role in your healing, and using the HOME Method as a way to embody self-love in your everyday life.

Why Self-Love Is Essential to Healing

At the core of any healing journey is the relationship you have with yourself. If you're constantly criticizing yourself, doubting your worth, or pushing yourself beyond your limits, healing becomes an uphill battle. Self-love, on the other hand, provides the fertile ground where healing can truly flourish. It gives you the permission to rest when you're tired, to forgive yourself when you stumble, and to pursue your dreams and goals without the burden of perfectionism.

Self-love allows you to approach life with a sense of compassion and care for your well-being. It's about treating yourself with the same kindness you would offer to a close friend or loved one. When you love yourself, you're more likely to make choices that align with your true needs rather than pushing yourself to meet external expectations or self-imposed pressures.

The Struggle with Self-Love: Why It's Hard to Love Ourselves

For many of us, loving ourselves feels like the hardest thing in the world. We're often our own harshest critics, carrying an internal dialogue that constantly points out where we fall short. We may have grown up with messages—whether from family, society, or even ourselves—that told us we weren't good enough, smart enough, pretty enough, or successful enough.

These beliefs can become deeply ingrained, making it difficult to access the unconditional love and acceptance that we all deserve. Self-love often requires us to unlearn these messages and confront the parts of ourselves that we've rejected or deemed unworthy. It's not about becoming perfect; it's about embracing your imperfections and recognizing that you are worthy of love and care exactly as you are.

Story: My Struggle with Self-Love

For much of my life, I struggled with self-love. I was constantly chasing external validation, believing that if I could just achieve more, be more, or look a certain way, I would finally feel good enough. I didn't realize that the root of my unhappiness wasn't in my external circumstances but in my inability to accept and love myself.

I spent years pushing myself to meet unrealistic standards, criticizing myself for every mistake, and feeling like I was never enough. It wasn't until I hit a point of deep burnout that I realized something had to change. I began to explore what it meant to truly love myself, and while the journey has been far from easy, it has been the most transformative part of my healing process. Self-love gave me permission to slow down, prioritize my well-being, and stop chasing perfection.

Step 1: Healing—Unlearning Self-Criticism and Embracing Self-Compassion

The first step in cultivating self-love is Healing the patterns of self-criticism and judgment that have been ingrained over time. Many of us have a harsh inner critic that tells us we're not good enough, smart enough, or worthy enough. This inner voice may have developed from past experiences—whether it was a critical parent, societal pressures, or our own unrealistic expectations.

Healing this relationship with yourself requires unlearning these patterns and replacing them with self-compassion. Self-compassion is the ability to treat yourself with kindness and understanding, even when you fall short of your expectations. It's recognizing that you are human, that mistakes are part of the journey, and that you deserve love and care, especially in difficult times.

Story: Learning to Be Compassionate with Myself

There was a time when I couldn't forgive myself for my mistakes. Every misstep felt like proof that I wasn't good enough. I would replay my failures over and over in my mind, judging myself harshly and feeling ashamed. This self-criticism became a heavy burden that made it nearly impossible for me to move forward.

It wasn't until I learned about self-compassion that I began to see a shift. I started practicing small acts of kindness toward myself—speaking to myself in a gentler tone, offering forgiveness when I made mistakes, and reminding myself that it's okay to be imperfect. Over time, this practice helped me heal the wounds that self-criticism had left behind, and it allowed me to approach life with more grace and acceptance.

Step 2: Observing—Noticing Your Inner Dialogue

The next step is Observing your inner dialogue. Pay attention to the way you speak to yourself throughout the day. Are you kind and supportive, or do you often criticize and judge yourself? The words you use in your self-talk have a powerful impact on how you feel about yourself and how you navigate the world.

Start by noticing when negative thoughts arise. Do you call yourself names, criticize your appearance, or judge your abilities? Becoming aware of these patterns is the first step to changing them. Once you observe your inner dialogue, you can begin to shift it from one of judgment to one of compassion and kindness.

Do You See This in Your Life?

- When you make a mistake, do you say things to yourself that you would never say to a friend?
- Do you have an ongoing mental script that tells you you're not good enough, smart enough, or attractive enough?
- Are you quick to dismiss your accomplishments, downplaying your successes or brushing off praise?
- Do you struggle to forgive yourself for past mistakes or shortcomings?

By observing these patterns, you can begin to replace them with more loving and supportive thoughts.

Step 3: Mindfulness—Practicing Self-Love in Daily Life

Once you've observed your inner dialogue, the next step is to bring Mindfulness to your self-love practice. Mindfulness involves being present with yourself, tuning into your emotions, and being aware of how you treat yourself in everyday situations. It's about being conscious of the way you respond to challenges, successes, and even ordinary moments.

Mindfulness helps you stay connected to your needs and feelings, allowing you to respond to yourself with care. When you notice feelings of stress, overwhelm, or self-doubt, mindfulness gives you the opportunity to pause, check in with yourself, and offer the love and support you need in that moment.

Story: Using Mindfulness to Practice Self-Love

One of the ways I began incorporating self-love into my life was through mindfulness. I started paying attention to how I was feeling throughout the day—whether I was stressed, tired, or feeling down—and I used those moments as opportunities to offer myself kindness. Instead of pushing through the discomfort or ignoring my needs, I would take a moment to ask myself, "What do I need right now?" Sometimes, it was a short break; other times, it was a reassuring word, and often, it was simply giving myself permission to slow down.

Through mindfulness, I learned to be more attuned to my inner world, and this awareness allowed me to care for myself in ways that I hadn't before. It wasn't always about doing something extravagant—it was about meeting myself where I was and offering what I needed in that moment.

Step 4: Embracing—Fully Committing to Self-Love

The final step is Embracing self-love as a non-negotiable part of your life. Loving yourself isn't something you do once and then forget about; it's an ongoing practice that requires commitment, especially during difficult times. It's about fully embracing who you are—your strengths, your flaws, and everything in between—and knowing that you are deserving of love, care, and respect no matter what.

Embracing self-love means making choices that support your well-being. It's about setting boundaries, prioritizing self-care, and honoring your needs, even when it feels uncomfortable. It's also about standing firm in the belief that you are worthy of love, not because of what you do or achieve, but simply because of who you are.

Story: Embracing Self-Love as a Lifelong Practice

When I first began practicing self-love, I thought it would be a quick fix—that once I learned to love myself, everything would fall into place. But I soon realized that self-love is a lifelong practice. There are days when it comes easily and other days when it's harder to access. The key is to keep showing up for yourself, even when it feels difficult.

Over time, I've learned to embrace self-love as an essential part of my life. It's no longer something I do only when things are going well; it's something I turn to in moments of struggle, doubt, and pain. This commitment to self-love has been one of the most transformative aspects of my healing journey, and it continues to shape how I move through the world.

Tools for Cultivating Self-Love

To help you cultivate self-love, here are some tools and reflective questions to guide you:

1. **Reframe Your Inner Dialogue**
   - Ask yourself: What would I say to a friend in this situation? How can I offer myself the same kindness and support?
   - When you notice self-critical thoughts, take a moment to reframe them. Replace harsh judgments with compassionate, supportive words. Treat yourself as you would a close friend.

2. **Practice Self-Compassion During Difficult Times**
   - Ask yourself: How can I be kind to myself as I navigate this challenge? What do I need in this moment to feel supported?
   - When you're going through a tough time, practice self-compassion by offering yourself understanding, patience, and care. Acknowledge that it's okay to struggle and that you deserve kindness, even when things are hard.

3. **Celebrate Your Wins, Big and Small**
   - Ask yourself: How can I honor my accomplishments and celebrate my progress?
   - Take time to celebrate your successes, no matter how small. Recognize your efforts, acknowledge your growth, and allow yourself to feel proud of how far you've come.

4.   Set Boundaries that Honor Your Well-Being

- Ask yourself: Where do I need to set boundaries to protect my energy and well-being?

- Setting boundaries is an act of self-love. Reflect on where you may need to establish or reinforce boundaries in your life to prioritize your mental, emotional, and physical health.

Exercise: Cultivating Self-Love Using the HOME Method

Here's an exercise to help you practice self-love using the HOME Method:

1.   **Healing:** Reflect on the areas of your life where you struggle with self-love. What old wounds or beliefs are keeping you from loving yourself fully? Write down one belief you can begin to heal (e.g., "I believe I'm only worthy of love when I'm perfect.").

2.   **Observing:** Pay attention to your inner dialogue. Notice when self-critical thoughts arise and observe how they make you feel. Begin to replace those thoughts with more loving and supportive words.

3.   **Mindfulness:** Practice staying present with yourself throughout the day. When you notice feelings of stress or overwhelm, check in with yourself and ask, "What do I need right now?" Offer yourself the love and care you need in that moment.

4.   **Embracing:** Fully commit to self-love as an ongoing practice. Embrace the idea that you are worthy of love, care, and compassion every day, regardless of your achievements or mistakes.

Self-Love Meditation: Embracing Yourself with Compassion

This self-love meditation is designed to help you reconnect with yourself, cultivate self-compassion, and deepen your sense of worthiness. You can do this meditation in a quiet, comfortable space where you won't be disturbed. Set aside 10-15 minutes for this practice, or longer if you feel drawn to spend more time with yourself.

Step 1: Find a Comfortable Position

- Sit in a comfortable position, either on a cushion or chair, with your spine straight and your hands resting gently in your lap.

- Close your eyes and take a deep breath in through your nose, allowing your lungs to fully expand. Exhale slowly through your mouth, releasing any tension or stress from the day.

- Continue to breathe naturally, allowing your body to relax with each exhale. Feel yourself becoming more present, grounded, and calm.

Step 2: Connect with Your Heart

- Bring your attention to the area around your heart, placing one hand gently on your chest if it feels right for you. Begin to breathe deeply into this space, imagining that each breath is softening and opening your heart.

- As you breathe, silently repeat the words: "I am open to love. I am open to receiving love." Allow these words to resonate within you, feeling your heart become more receptive to self-compassion.

Step 3: Invite Self-Love

- Now, bring to mind something about yourself that you've been struggling with—a mistake, a perceived flaw, or an area where you've been hard on yourself lately. Hold this thought gently, as though you were holding a delicate object in your hands.

- Imagine wrapping this thought in warmth and kindness as though you're offering it compassion rather than judgment. Silently repeat the words: "I forgive myself. I love myself exactly as I am." Continue breathing deeply as you offer yourself this compassion.

- If feelings of resistance arise, acknowledge them without judgment. Simply observe them, and then return to the words: "I love myself exactly as I am." Let yourself soften into these words.

Step 4: Visualize a Light of Love

- Imagine a warm, golden light forming in the center of your heart. With each breath, this light begins to expand, growing brighter and larger. See this light as a symbol of the unconditional love you hold for yourself.

- Allow this golden light to fill your entire chest, then gradually spread to the rest of your body. Feel it move through your arms, legs, and head until every part of you is bathed in this light.

- As this light fills you, silently affirm: "I am worthy of love. I deserve kindness and compassion. I love myself fully." Let these affirmations sink in as you continue to breathe, letting the warmth of self-love fill your entire being.

Step 5: Embrace the Present Moment

- Stay with this feeling of warmth and love for a few more breaths. If your mind begins to wander, gently bring your focus back to your breath and the golden light surrounding you.

- As you sit in this space of love, remind yourself that you are exactly where you need to be and that you are worthy of love at every stage of your journey.

- Silently repeat the words: "I am enough. I am deserving of love. I honor myself with compassion." Allow these words to resonate deeply within you.

Step 6: Closing the Meditation

- When you feel ready, slowly begin to bring your awareness back to the room. Take a few deep breaths and gently wiggle your fingers and toes, feeling yourself becoming more grounded.

- Before opening your eyes, take a moment to thank yourself for taking the time to nurture and love yourself. Silently affirm: "I carry this love with me throughout my day." Feel the gratitude for this practice and the love you've cultivated for yourself.

- When you're ready, open your eyes slowly, carrying this feeling of self-love with you as you return to your day.

After the Meditation: Carrying Self-Love with You

Following this meditation, take a few moments to reflect on how you feel. How did it feel to offer yourself love and compassion? Were there any moments of resistance or discomfort? If so, know that this is a normal part of the process and that you can return to this practice anytime to deepen your connection with self-love.

Consider journaling about your experience or writing down any thoughts or insights that came to you during the meditation. Over time, this practice can help you cultivate a deeper sense of love and acceptance for yourself, making it easier to carry that love with you throughout your day.

This self-love meditation can be done regularly to strengthen your relationship with yourself, allowing you to move through life with more compassion, kindness, and self-acceptance.

Affirmations for Cultivating Self-Love

Here are some affirmations to help you develop self-love:

1. I am worthy of love and care, exactly as I am.
2. I treat myself with kindness and compassion, even when I make mistakes.
3. I honor my needs and prioritize my well-being.
4. I release self-criticism and embrace self-compassion.
5. I celebrate my growth and progress, no matter how small.
6. I set boundaries that protect my energy and well-being.

7.   I forgive myself for past mistakes and allow myself to grow from them.

8.   I am deserving of love, not because of what I do, but because of who I am.

9.   I am patient with myself as I heal, grow, and evolve.

10. I fully embrace myself—my strengths, my flaws, and everything in between.

Chapter 17

Boundaries as Acts of Self-Respect—Creating Space for Your Well-Being

Introduction: The Importance of Boundaries

Setting boundaries is one of the most powerful and necessary acts of self-care and self-respect. Boundaries aren't about shutting people out or being selfish; they're about protecting your emotional, mental, and physical well-being. When you set healthy boundaries, you create the space needed to thrive, grow, and be your authentic self without being drained, overwhelmed, or manipulated by others.

For many of us, however, boundaries can feel challenging to establish, especially if we've been raised to put others' needs before our own. We might worry that setting boundaries will make us appear selfish, unkind, or unloving. But the truth is that boundaries allow us to love ourselves and others more fully. They prevent resentment, burnout, and unhealthy dynamics by ensuring that our needs are met in ways that honor our well-being.

In this chapter, we'll explore the power of boundaries, why they are essential for your mental and emotional health, how to create visual boundaries, and how to use the HOME Method to set and maintain them with clarity and confidence.

What Are Boundaries and Why Do We Need Them?

Boundaries are the limits we set for ourselves in relationships, work, and daily life to protect our energy, emotional health, and sense of self. These limits define what is acceptable and what is not, allowing us to communicate clearly with others about our needs, values, and expectations.

Boundaries come in many forms, including:

- **Physical Boundaries:** Defining your personal space, privacy, and physical needs.

- **Emotional Boundaries:** Protect your emotional well-being by managing how much emotional energy you invest in others and deciding how much of your feelings and

- vulnerabilities to share.

- **Mental Boundaries:** Defending your thoughts, opinions, and beliefs from external pressures or invalidation.

- **Time Boundaries:** Managing how you spend your time and ensuring that others respect it.

- **Energy Boundaries:** Recognizing when you're overextending yourself and preserving your energy for what matters most.

Without healthy boundaries, we risk feeling depleted, resentful, or even taken advantage of. Boundaries help us maintain balance, create healthy relationships, and ensure that we're not sacrificing our well-being to meet the demands or expectations of others.

Why Setting Boundaries Can Be Difficult

For many of us, setting boundaries can feel uncomfortable or even frightening. We may have been taught that saying "no" is wrong, selfish, or hurtful. We might fear conflict or rejection if we express our limits, or we may worry that others will think less of us if we prioritize our own needs. These fears often stem from past experiences or societal conditioning that values self-sacrifice over self-care.

Additionally, if we've been in relationships where our boundaries were repeatedly crossed, it can be hard to trust that setting boundaries will be respected. This makes the act of boundary-setting feel risky or futile.

Story: My Journey with Setting Boundaries

For most of my life, I struggled with setting boundaries, especially in relationships. I was a chronic people-pleaser, always putting others' needs before my own, even when it left me feeling exhausted or resentful. I was afraid that if I said "no" or expressed my limits, people would see me as difficult or selfish, and I feared losing their approval.

But over time, I realized that not setting boundaries was costing me my mental and emotional well-being. I was drained, overwhelmed, and constantly compromising my needs to make others happy. It wasn't until I hit a point of burnout that I finally understood the importance of boundaries. I started small—saying no to requests that felt too draining, creating space for myself when I needed it, and being honest about my needs. While it was uncomfortable at first, setting boundaries has been one of the most empowering and transformative practices in my life.

Step 1: Healing—Letting Go of the Fear of Disappointing Others

The first step in setting healthy boundaries is Healing the fear of disappointing or upsetting others. Many of us avoid setting boundaries because we don't want to hurt anyone's feelings or we worry that others will reject us if we don't meet their expectations. But holding onto this fear keeps us stuck in unhealthy dynamics, where our needs are consistently pushed aside.

Healing this fear involves recognizing that you are not responsible for other people's feelings or reactions. Setting boundaries is an act of self-care, not selfishness. It's about honoring your well-being and trusting that those who truly respect and care for you will honor your boundaries as well.

Story: Healing My Fear of Conflict

For a long time, I avoided setting boundaries because I was terrified of conflict. I believed that if I expressed my needs or said "no," it would lead to confrontation, and I didn't want to risk the discomfort of that. But over time, I realized that avoiding conflict was costing me my peace of mind. I was allowing others to cross my boundaries because I feared their reactions, but in the process, I was betraying myself.

Healing this fear meant learning to be okay with the possibility of disappointment or disagreement. I started to understand that conflict didn't mean the end of a relationship or that I was unkind. It simply meant that I was standing up for myself, and that's something I could do with love and respect. As I healed this fear, I found that setting boundaries became easier, and my relationships improved because they were built on mutual respect.

Step 2: Observing—Noticing Where Your Boundaries Are Being Crossed

The next step is Observing where your boundaries are currently being crossed or where they need to be strengthened. Take some time to reflect on the relationships or situations in your life where you feel drained, resentful, or overwhelmed. These are often signs that your boundaries need attention.

Ask yourself:

- Do I often feel taken advantage of in certain relationships?
- Are there times when I say "yes" to things I don't want to do just to avoid conflict or guilt?
- Do I feel like I don't have enough time for myself because I'm always meeting others' needs?
- Are there people in my life who regularly disregard my feelings, space, or time?

By observing where your boundaries are being crossed, you can begin to identify the areas in your life where you need to set clearer limits.

Step 3: Mindfulness—Visualizing and Communicating Your Boundaries

Mindfulness in boundary-setting involves being intentional and aware when communicating your limits to others. But sometimes, we also need a more tangible or visual reminder of our boundaries—especially in situations where we feel emotionally vulnerable or energetically drained. One helpful tool is the practice of visualizing a boundary around yourself, creating a safe and sacred space wherever you go.

Visualization Tool: Creating Your Imaginary Ring

Imagine that you are surrounded by a protective ring or circle. This ring represents your personal boundary—it's invisible to others, but for you, it serves as a reminder that your space, energy, and well-being are protected. You can visualize this ring as a soft glow of light, a shield, or even a wall, depending on what feels most protective and nurturing to you.

Whenever you feel overwhelmed, overextended, or need a reminder of your boundaries, close your eyes and visualize this protective ring. Breathe deeply and imagine that this boundary is keeping you safe, filtering out negative energy or unwanted demands while allowing in only what nourishes and supports you.

You can use this visualization before entering difficult conversations, stressful environments, or situations where your boundaries are likely to be tested. It serves as a tangible reminder of your right to protect your energy and space.

Example: Using the Ring Visualization for Emotional Boundaries

I began using the ring visualization when I noticed how easily I absorbed the emotions of others, particularly in stressful situations. I would often leave conversations feeling drained or overwhelmed, especially when I was dealing with people who were emotionally demanding. One day, before a difficult conversation, I visualized a soft, glowing ring around me—a boundary that would allow me to stay compassionate without taking on the other person's emotional weight.

Throughout the conversation, I checked in with my boundaries and reminded myself that I was protected. The visualization helped me maintain emotional clarity and leave the interaction feeling much more grounded and centered.

Step 4: Embracing—Honoring Your Boundaries as Acts of Self-Respect

The final step is Embracing your boundaries as an essential acts of self-respect. Boundaries are not just about protecting yourself from others—they're about affirming your worth and prioritizing your well-being. When you set boundaries, you're sending a message to yourself and to others that your time, energy, and emotional health matter.

Embracing boundaries means releasing any guilt or shame you may feel about saying no or asserting your needs. It's about recognizing that setting limits is an act of love, both for yourself and for those around you. By honoring your boundaries, you create healthier relationships built on respect, trust, and mutual understanding.

Story: Embracing Boundaries as a Form of Self-Respect

For years, I struggled with setting boundaries because I felt guilty. I believed that saying no meant I was letting people down or being unkind. But over time, I realized that constantly overextending myself was not only harming me but also creating resentment in my relationships. I was giving more than I had to give, and it left me feeling depleted.

Once I began embracing boundaries as acts of self-respect, everything changed. I no longer felt guilty for protecting my time and energy. I started to see boundaries not as walls but as tools for creating healthier connections—both with myself and with others. Embracing boundaries allowed me to show up more fully and authentically in my relationships, and it deepened my sense of self-worth.

Tools for Setting and Maintaining Boundaries

Here are some tools and reflective questions to help you set and maintain boundaries:

1. **Reflect on Your Needs**
   - Ask yourself: What do I need to feel supported, respected, and emotionally safe in my relationships and daily life?
   - Start by identifying your core needs in different areas of your life—whether it's time for yourself, respect for your emotions, or space to pursue your own goals.

2. **Practice Saying No**
   - Ask yourself: How can I say no with clarity and kindness?
   - Practice saying no in situations where you feel overextended or uncomfortable. It's okay to decline requests or invitations that don't align with your needs or priorities.

3. **Visualize Your Personal Boundary**

- Ask yourself: What does my personal boundary look like? How can I use this visualization to stay grounded and protected?

- Use the ring visualization whenever you feel vulnerable or need a tangible reminder of your boundaries. Picture yourself surrounded by a protective circle that honors your space, energy, and well-being.

4. **Set Boundaries Without Apology**

- Ask yourself: Am I apologizing for setting boundaries? How can I communicate with them more confidently?

- When you set boundaries, avoid apologizing or justifying your needs. Stand firm in your limits with confidence and trust that you deserve to be respected.

Exercise: Strengthening Your Boundaries Using the HOME Method

Here's an exercise to help you set and maintain boundaries using the HOME Method:

1. **Healing:** Reflect on any fears or guilt you have around setting boundaries. Are you afraid of disappointing others or being seen as unkind? Write down one belief you can begin to heal (e.g., "I believe that saying no makes me selfish.").

2. **Observing:** Notice where your boundaries are currently being crossed. Are there certain relationships or situations where you feel drained or resentful? Identify where you need to set clearer limits.

3. **Mindfulness:** Practice mindfulness the next time you need to set a boundary. Take a moment to check in with yourself before responding to a request or situation. Visualize your protective ring, and communicate your boundary clearly and kindly, without guilt or apology.

4. **Embracing:** Embrace your boundaries as acts of self-respect. Trust that setting limits is a way to honor your worth and create healthier relationships.

Affirmations for Setting and Honoring Boundaries

Here are some affirmations to help you set and honor boundaries with confidence:

1. I have the right to set boundaries that protect my well-being.

2. I communicate my boundaries with clarity and confidence.

3. I release guilt and embrace my needs as valid and important.

4. I respect my energy and time by saying no when necessary.

5. My boundaries are acts of self-love and self-respect.

6. I deserve relationships that honor my limits and needs.

7. I release the fear of disappointing others and honor my boundaries without apology.

8. I trust that setting boundaries creates healthier, more balanced relationships.

9. I am worthy of respect, and my boundaries reflect that worth.

10. I create space for my well-being by maintaining clear and healthy boundaries.

Chapter 18

The Art of Letting Go—Releasing What No Longer Serves You

Introduction: The Power of Letting Go

Letting go is one of the most challenging and liberating acts we can undertake on our journey toward healing and growth. It's the act of releasing attachments to people, situations, habits, and beliefs that no longer serve us. Whether it's the emotional weight of past hurts, a relationship that has run its course, or a limiting belief that keeps you stuck, letting go creates space for new experiences, new growth, and new possibilities to enter your life.

In this chapter, we'll explore the art of letting go, why it's so difficult, how to release what no longer serves us, and include symbolic ceremonies you can use to help with this process. These simple but powerful rituals can create a tangible experience of release, allowing you to let go with greater clarity and intention.

Why Letting Go Is So Difficult

Letting go is often difficult because it involves loss—whether that's the loss of a relationship, a familiar routine, or an identity we've held onto for years. We may fear that letting go will leave us feeling empty or lost, unsure of what will take its place. This fear can cause us to hold on tightly to things, even when they are no longer healthy or fulfilling.

Another reason letting go is challenging is that we tend to associate it with failure. We might feel that if we let go of a goal or a relationship, it means we've failed. But letting go is not about giving up—it's about recognizing when something is no longer serving your highest good and having the courage to release it with love and trust.

Story: My Struggle with Letting Go of My Business

For years, I poured my heart and soul into building my own business. It was more than just a job—it was my identity, my passion, and my dream. I had invested countless hours, emotions, and energy into making it work. But over time, the stress of running everything on my own, the uncertainty of income, and the constant pressure began to wear me down. My business, which once brought me joy, started to feel like a heavy burden.

The thought of letting it go felt like admitting defeat. I feared that closing my business would mean I had failed and that I wasn't capable of succeeding as an entrepreneur. But deep down, I knew it was time to make a change. I could feel that holding on to it was draining me, and I wasn't able to be fully present in other areas of my life.

Letting go of my business was one of the hardest decisions I've ever made. I took a leap of faith and accepted a full-time job working for someone else's company. It felt strange at first—like I was giving up my independence. But as I settled into my new role, I began to see the freedom that came with it. I no longer had to carry the weight of running everything by myself. I had more time for self-care, for relationships, and for exploring new passions. Letting go of my business wasn't a failure—it was a necessary step toward reclaiming balance in my life.

What We Hold On To—and Why

We hold onto many things—relationships, beliefs, fears, and even physical possessions—because they give us a sense of security or identity. But over time, these attachments can weigh us down, making it harder to move forward. Here are a few common things we hold on to and why they can be difficult to release:

- **Past Hurts and Resentments:** Holding onto past pain can feel like a way to protect ourselves from being hurt again, but it often keeps us stuck in a cycle of negativity and prevents us from healing.

- **Unhealthy Relationships:** We may hold onto relationships out of fear of being alone or because we feel obligated to maintain connections, even when they're toxic or draining.

- **Limiting Beliefs:** These are the stories we tell ourselves about what we can or cannot do.

- They may have served us at one point, but they can keep us from pursuing new opportunities or stepping into our true potential.

- **Perfectionism and Control:** The need to control outcomes or achieve perfection can be a heavy burden, preventing us from enjoying the present moment or accepting ourselves as we are.

Step 1: Healing—Releasing the Need to Control

The first step in letting go is Healing the need to control outcomes or hold onto things that no longer serve us. Control often gives us a false sense of security, but it can keep us stuck in unhealthy patterns. We may believe that by holding onto people, habits, or situations, we can prevent pain or avoid the unknown.

But healing requires us to trust that we don't need to have all the answers or control every detail. Letting go means accepting that life is full of uncertainty and that sometimes, we need to release the old to make room for the new.

Story: Letting Go of My Need for Perfection

For years, I struggled with perfectionism. I believed that if I could control every detail of my life and achieve perfection, I would be safe from failure, disappointment, or criticism. But this constant need for control left me feeling anxious and overwhelmed, and no matter how much I accomplished, it never felt like enough.

The turning point came when I realized that perfection was an impossible standard. I had been holding on to an unrealistic expectation that was causing me stress and robbing me of joy.

Learning to let go of perfectionism wasn't easy—it required me to face my fear of failure and embrace my imperfections. But as I slowly released my need for control, I found more peace and acceptance within myself.

Step 2: Observing—Identifying What No Longer Serves You

The next step is Observing what you are holding onto that no longer serves your growth or well-being. This requires honest reflection. Take time to examine the relationships, habits, beliefs, or patterns in your life that feel heavy, draining, or out of alignment with who you are becoming.

Ask yourself:

- Are there relationships in my life that feel toxic or one-sided?

- Am I holding onto beliefs or fears that keep me from pursuing my dreams?

- Are there habits or routines that drain my energy or keep me stuck in the past?

- Am I holding onto resentment or pain from past experiences that I haven't fully healed?

By observing what no longer serves you, you can begin to make conscious decisions about what to release.

Do You See This in Your Life?

- Do you continue to stay in relationships out of fear, obligation, or guilt, even when they leave you feeling emotionally exhausted?

- Are there limiting beliefs that keep you from trying something new, like pursuing a dream or stepping outside your comfort zone?

- Do you hold onto anger or resentment toward someone, replaying past hurts in your mind, even though it causes you pain?

Recognizing these patterns is the first step in letting go.

Step 3: Mindfulness—Letting Go with Awareness

Once you've identified what you need to release, the next step is Mindfulness. Mindfulness helps you let go with awareness and compassion rather than reacting impulsively or out of fear. It allows you to observe the process of letting go without judgment, acknowledging the emotions that come up and allowing them to pass.

Mindfulness also helps you stay present during the process of release. Letting go can stir up feelings of grief, fear, or uncertainty, but mindfulness teaches you to sit with these emotions and trust that they are part of the process.

Story: Using Mindfulness to Let Go of a Relationship

Letting go of a long-term friendship was one of the hardest things I've done. The relationship had become toxic, but because we had so much history, I felt guilty about ending it. I kept holding on, hoping things would get better, but each interaction left me feeling drained.

I decided to approach the situation with mindfulness. Instead of rushing to end the relationship out of anger, I took time to reflect on how it was affecting my emotional well-being. I practiced sitting with the discomfort of letting go and allowed myself to feel the sadness and fear that came with it. Over time, I found the strength to release the friendship, not out of resentment but from a place of compassion—for both myself and the other person.

Step 4: Embracing—Trusting the Process of Release

The final step is Embracing the process of letting go. Letting go is not a one-time act—it's a continuous process that requires trust and patience. When we let go, we often have to sit with the uncertainty of what comes next. But by embracing the process, we create space for new opportunities, relationships, and experiences to flow into our lives.

Trust that letting go is a necessary part of growth. Just as trees shed their leaves in autumn to prepare for new growth in spring, we, too, must release what no longer serves us to make room for what is meant for us.

Story: Embracing the Uncertainty After Letting Go of My Business

Letting go of my business and taking a full-time job was one of the hardest decisions I've ever made. My business had been my identity for so long that I wasn't sure who I would be without it. I feared that working for someone else would feel like a loss of freedom and creativity.

But after making the decision to let go, I began to feel a sense of relief. No longer burdened by the stress of running everything on my own, I found that I had more time and energy for other things in my life. I was able to focus on self-care, spend more time with loved ones, and even rediscover passions I had forgotten about. Letting go of my business wasn't the end—it was a new beginning that brought unexpected growth and fulfillment.

Symbolic Ceremonies for Letting Go

Sometimes, it's helpful to create a symbolic ceremony to mark the act of letting go. These ceremonies can make the process feel more tangible, giving you a physical representation of release. Here are a few simple but powerful ceremonies to help you let go with intention.

1.   Writing and Tearing the Past Away

One of the most effective symbolic acts is writing down what you need to release and then tearing the paper into pieces as a physical representation of letting it go.

- Take a piece of paper and write down everything you want to release—old beliefs, resentment, fears, or relationships that no longer serve you.

- As you write, allow yourself to feel the emotions that come up. Acknowledge the weight of what you've been carrying.

- When you're ready, tear the paper into small pieces, symbolizing your decision to release these burdens. As you do, repeat an affirmation such as: "I release what no longer serves me with love and gratitude."

- Dispose of the pieces in a way that feels right to you—burn them (safely), throw them away, or scatter them in nature. As you do, visualize the weight being lifted from your shoulders.

Tools for Letting Go with the HOME Method

Here are some tools and reflective questions to help you practice the art of letting go:

1.   Reflect on What No Longer Serves You

- Ask yourself: What am I holding onto that is no longer aligned with my growth?

- Reflect on the relationships, habits, beliefs, or fears that feel heavy or draining. Write them down and consider why you are still holding onto them.

2. **Practice the Art of Release**

- Ask yourself: How can I let go with grace and compassion?

- Instead of forcing yourself to let go, approach it with mindfulness and compassion.

Acknowledge the emotions that come up, and allow yourself to release them gently over time.

3. **Visualize the Release**

- Ask yourself: What would it feel like to release this from my life?

- Use visualization to help you let go. Picture yourself releasing the person, belief, or habit with love. Imagine it floating away, leaving you lighter and more open to what's next.

4. **Embrace the Uncertainty**

- Ask yourself: What new possibilities can emerge when I let go?

- Embrace the unknown with trust. Letting go can create space for new opportunities to enter your life. Reflect on the possibilities that could unfold once you release what is no longer serving you.

Exercise: Letting Go Using the HOME Method

Here's an exercise to help you practice letting go using the HOME Method:

1. **Healing:** Reflect on your need for control. What fears or beliefs are keeping you from letting go? Write down one belief you can begin to heal (e.g., "I believe that if I let go, I will lose something important.").

2. **Observing:** Notice what you are holding onto. Identify the relationships, beliefs, or habits that feel heavy or out of alignment with your well-being.

3. **Mindfulness:** Practice mindful release. Sit with the emotions that arise as you let go, and observe them without judgment. Allow yourself to feel the discomfort, but trust that it will pass.

4. **Embracing:** Embrace the process of letting go as an act of growth. Trust that by releasing what no longer serves you, you are creating space for new experiences and opportunities to enter your life.

Affirmations for Letting Go

Here are some affirmations to help you practice letting go with grace and trust:

1. I release what no longer serves me with love and gratitude.

2. I trust that letting go creates space for new opportunities to flow into my life.

3. I am safe in the unknown, and I trust the process of life.

4. I release the need to control outcomes and embrace the present moment.

5.   I forgive myself and others, and I release the past with peace.

6.   I am worthy of new beginnings, and I embrace change with an open heart.

7.   I trust that what is meant for me will find me in its own time.

8.   I let go of limiting beliefs and welcome new possibilities.

9.   I release resentment and make space for healing and peace.

10.   I trust that letting go brings me closer to my highest self.

Chapter 19

Stepping Into Your Authentic Self—Living in Alignment with Who You Truly Are

Introduction: The Journey Toward Authenticity

At the heart of every healing journey lies the desire to live in alignment with your true, authentic self. Authenticity means showing up in the world as who you genuinely are—without masks, without fear of judgment, and without the pressure to conform to others' expectations. It's about embracing your unique qualities, quirks, and values and living from a place of truth, even when it's uncomfortable.

Stepping into your authentic self requires courage. For many of us, we've spent years—or even a lifetime—wearing different masks to fit in, to be liked, or to avoid rejection. But the cost of hiding who we truly are is high: we feel disconnected from ourselves, we attract relationships that don't truly fulfil us, and we may even feel like we're living someone else's life.

But remember when we discussed the feeling of home as the place where you feel safe enough to be yourself? Where you don't need to wear masks or costumes, where you can fully show up as you are? We've travelled through the process of discovering who we thought we were—the identity shaped by external expectations and old conditioning. Now, it's time to arrive at your true destination—home—which is, in essence, your authentic self. This chapter is about finding and becoming that authentic self. We'll explore how the HOME

Method can help you align your actions, choices, and relationships with the truest version of you.

Why We Struggle to Be Authentic

Many of us struggle to be authentic because we've been taught—consciously or unconsciously—that our true selves aren't enough. As children, we may have received messages from parents, teachers, or peers that told us we had to behave a certain way to be loved, accepted, or successful. Over time, these messages become internalized, and we start to shape our identities based on who we think we need to be rather than who we truly are.

As adults, this pressure to conform doesn't necessarily go away. We might still feel the need to wear masks in our relationships, our careers, or even within our families out of fear of judgment or rejection. But living inauthentically can create deep inner conflict. It can manifest as anxiety, depression, or a persistent sense of dissatisfaction with life.

Story: My Struggle with Authenticity

For much of my life, I struggled with the fear of being truly seen. I was always adapting to what I thought others wanted me to be—whether in friendships, relationships, or work environments. I believed that if I could mold myself into the "right" version of, I would be loved, accepted, and successful. But the more I did this, the more disconnected I felt from my true self. I started to notice that I wasn't living my life for me—I was living it based on what I thought I should be, and it was exhausting.

The turning point came when I realized that I could no longer keep up the facade. It wasn't easy, and it didn't happen overnight. But little by little, I began to strip away the masks. I started saying "no" to things that didn't align with my values. I stopped trying to please everyone. And most importantly, I gave myself permission to show up as me—flaws, quirks, and all.

The more I embraced my authentic self, the more aligned my life became. I started to attract relationships, opportunities, and experiences that were truly meant for me rather than the ones I had been chasing out of fear. And while it's still a journey, stepping into my authentic self has been one of the most liberating and empowering decisions I've ever made.

What It Means to Live Authentically

Living authentically means living in alignment with your values, your truth, and your unique purpose. It's about making decisions that reflect who you truly are rather than who you think you should be. Here are a few key aspects of authenticity:

- **Honesty:** Being honest with yourself and others about your feelings, needs, and boundaries.
- **Vulnerability:** Allowing yourself to be open and vulnerable, even when it feels uncomfortable or risky.
- **Integrity:** Living in a way that is consistent with your values and beliefs, even when it goes against the expectations of others.
- **Courage:** Having the courage to follow your own path, even when it feels uncertain or unpopular.

- **Self-Acceptance:** Embracing all parts of yourself—the parts you love and the parts you are still working on—without shame or judgment.

The Masks We Wear—and Why

As we discussed earlier in the book, many of us wear masks to protect ourselves. We might put on a mask of perfection, pretending we have it all together, when inside, we feel overwhelmed. We might wear the mask of the people-pleaser, saying yes to everything and everyone while our true desires are buried deep inside. We might even wear the mask of the strong one, never showing our vulnerability, afraid that others will see us as weak.

These masks serve a purpose—they protect us from feeling exposed or rejected. But they also disconnect us from our true selves and from others. When we hide behind these masks, we prevent authentic connection. We attract relationships, jobs, and experiences that are a reflection of the mask, not who we really are. And over time, the weight of wearing these masks becomes unbearable.

Story: Letting Go of the Perfection Mask

For years, I wore the mask of perfection. I believed that if I could just be perfect in everything I did, I would be safe from criticism or failure. I was always striving to be the best at work, in relationships, and in how I presented myself to the world. But this constant striving for perfection came at a cost. I was exhausted, anxious, and never felt good enough, no matter how hard I tried.

Eventually, I reached a breaking point. I realized that I couldn't keep up the facade of perfection any longer. I had to let go of the need to be perfect and allow myself to be human. It was scary at first—letting others see my flaws, my mistakes, and my vulnerabilities. But as I peeled away the perfection mask, I began to experience deeper connections with others and, most importantly, with myself.

Step 1: Healing—Letting Go of Who You Think You Should Be

The first step in stepping into your authentic self is Healing the need to be who you think you should be. Many of us carry deep-rooted beliefs that tell us we need to be a certain way to be loved or accepted. These beliefs often come from childhood experiences, societal conditioning, or past relationships where we felt we had to change to fit in.

Healing requires us to question these beliefs and let go of the idea that we need to be perfect, people-pleasing, or "good enough" to be worthy of love. It's about embracing the idea that you are enough exactly as you are and that your authentic self is more than worthy of being seen and celebrated.

Story: Letting Go of People-Pleasing

For much of my life, I was a people-pleaser. I would go out of my way to make sure everyone else was happy, even if it meant neglecting my own needs. I believed that if I could just make everyone around me happy, they would love me. But what I didn't realize was that by constantly pleasing others, I was abandoning myself.

Healing from people-pleasing meant learning to set boundaries and say no, even when it was uncomfortable. It meant letting go of the fear of disappointing others and trusting that my needs were just as important. The more I let go of the need to please, the more I began to see that true connection comes from authenticity, not from being everything to everyone.

Step 2: Observing—Noticing When You're Wearing a Mask

The next step is Observing when you're wearing a mask. Take a moment to reflect on the areas of your life where you might be hiding your true self. Do you feel like you have to put on a certain persona at work, in your relationships, or even around your family? Are there moments when you feel like you're performing or pretending rather than being real?

Observing these patterns can help you identify where you need to make changes and start showing up more authentically. It's important to observe without judgment—wearing masks is a protective mechanism we've all used at some point. But recognizing where you're hiding is the first step in reclaiming your true self.

Do You See This in Your Life?

- Do you say yes to things you don't really want to do just to avoid conflict or rejection?
- Do you feel like you have to be the "strong one" in your relationships, never showing your vulnerability?
- Are there areas of your life where you feel like you're "playing a role" rather than being yourself?

Once you start observing these patterns, you can begin to take steps toward living more authentically.

Step 3: Mindfulness—Connecting with Your True Self

The next step is Mindfulness—taking the time to connect with your true self. Mindfulness allows you to become aware of your thoughts, feelings and desires in the present moment without judgment. It helps you tune into what you truly want and need rather than what others expect from you.

Mindfulness can also help you notice when you're slipping back into old patterns of wearing masks or people-pleasing. By staying present, you can make conscious choices about how you want to show up in the world.

Story: Using Mindfulness to Stay Authentic

There was a time when I would automatically say yes to every request, even when I didn't want to. I would agree to social events, projects, or commitments that didn't align with my true desires simply because I didn't want to let anyone down. But through mindfulness, I began to slow down and check in with myself before responding. I started asking myself, "Is this what I truly want? Am I saying yes out of obligation or fear?"

The more I practiced mindfulness, the more I was able to make decisions that were aligned with my true self. I started saying no to things that didn't feel right and yes to the things that brought me joy. This practice allowed me to show up more authentically, not just for others but for myself.

Step 4: Embracing—Living in Alignment with Your Authentic Self

The final step is Embracing your authentic self. This means fully accepting who you are without shame or apology. It's about letting go of the need to conform and trusting that when you show up as your true self, you attract the right people, opportunities, and experiences into your life.

Embracing authenticity is a lifelong journey—it's not something you achieve once and for all. But the more you practice living in alignment with who you truly are, the more peace, joy, and fulfilment you will experience.

Story: Embracing My Authentic Self

When I finally embraced my authentic self, I started to feel a deep sense of inner peace. I no longer felt the need to hide behind masks or play roles to fit in. I gave myself permission to be vulnerable, to say no when something didn't align with my values, and to pursue the things that truly lit me up. The more I embraced who I really was, the more I noticed that my relationships and experiences became richer and more meaningful.

Tools for Stepping Into Your Authentic Self

Here are some tools and reflective questions to help you step into your authentic self using the HOME Method:

1.   **Reflect on Who You've Been Trying to Be**
     - Ask yourself: Who have I been trying to be to gain love or acceptance?

- Reflect on the personas or masks you've worn throughout your life. What expectations have you been trying to live up to, and how have these shaped your identity?

2. **Observe When You're Not Being Authentic**

- Ask yourself: When do I feel like I'm pretending or performing?
- Notice the areas of your life where you feel like you're not being true to yourself.

Observe these moments with curiosity, and ask yourself how you can show up more authentically.

3. **Practice Mindfulness in Your Choices**

- Ask yourself: Is this decision aligned with my true self?
- Use mindfulness to check in with yourself before making decisions. Are you saying yes out of obligation or fear or because it truly aligns with who you are?

4. **Embrace Vulnerability**

- Ask yourself: What would it look like to show up fully as myself?
- Embrace the courage to be vulnerable and let others see the real you. Trust that by being authentic, you create deeper connections and attract experiences that are aligned with your true self.

Exercise: Becoming Your Authentic Self Using the HOME Method

Here's an exercise to help you step into your authentic self using the HOME Method:

1. **Healing:** Reflect on the old beliefs that have kept you from being your true self. Write down one belief you can begin to heal (e.g., "I have to be perfect to be loved.").

2. **Observing:** Notice when you're wearing a mask. Identify the areas in your life where you feel like you're pretending or playing a role, and observe how it makes you feel.

3. **Mindfulness:** Practice staying mindful of your choices. Before responding to requests or making decisions, ask yourself if they are aligned with your authentic self.

4. **Embracing:** Embrace the courage to live in alignment with your true self. Trust that by showing up authentically, you are creating a life that is more fulfilling and aligned with who you really are.

Affirmations for Authenticity

Here are some affirmations to help you step into your authentic self:

1. I am worthy of being seen and loved for who I truly am.

2. I release the need to wear masks and embrace my true self.

3. I live in alignment with my values and my truth.

4. I have the courage to show up authentically, even when it's uncomfortable.

5.   I trust that by being myself, I attract the right people and opportunities into my life.

6.   I embrace my vulnerability as a strength, not a weakness.

7.   I no longer seek validation from others; I validate myself.

8.   I am enough exactly as I am.

9.   I trust that my authentic self is worthy of love, acceptance, and respect.

10.   I let go of the need to conform and step fully into my true power.

Chapter 20

Coming Home—Embracing the Journey of Healing and Growth

Introduction: The Full Circle

As we arrive at the final chapter, it's time to reflect on the journey we've traveled together. From understanding what it means to seek "home"—not as a physical place but as an emotional, spiritual destination—we've explored healing, self-awareness, mindfulness, and ultimately embracing our authentic selves. The HOME Method has been our guiding star, leading us back to a deeper understanding of what it means to truly come home to ourselves.

But here's the truth that this journey has revealed: coming home isn't about reaching a specific point where everything is perfect or resolved. It's about realizing that you are your home. This final chapter is about integrating everything we've learned, knowing that coming home is not a final destination. Instead, it's a continuous process of unfolding, of returning to yourself again and again with love, acceptance, and grace.

What It Means to Come Home

Coming home means something much deeper than simply finding peace. It's a profound return to the essence of who you are. It's recognizing that, despite all of life's challenges, uncertainties, and twists, you are your safest place, your sanctuary, your source of inner peace.

When you truly come home, you realize:

- **You Are Enough:** There's no more striving to be someone you're not, no more chasing approval or validation from others. You embrace the fullness of who you are, flaws and all, and trust that you are enough exactly as you are.

- **The Journey Is the Destination:** Rather than seeking an endpoint where everything is perfect, you understand that growth, learning, and healing will always be part of the path. The process of becoming your true self is the journey home.

- **You Carry Peace Within:** No matter what happens in the external world, you can return to the peace and stillness that reside within you. This inner sense of home is your constant, your anchor in the ever-changing tides of life.

- **Authenticity Is Your Compass:** Living in alignment with who you truly are—your values, desires, and truth—becomes your north star. You trust that when you live in this place, everything else falls into place.

My Own Journey Home

Reflecting on my own journey, I now realize that, for much of my life, I was searching for "home" in all the wrong places. I thought that if I achieved enough, proved myself enough, or earned enough validation, I would feel secure. I believed that home was somewhere "out there"—in the opinions of others, in success, in approval.

But the truth is, I wasn't seeking those things at all. What I was really searching for was me. I wanted to come home to myself, to feel safe, whole, and enough, exactly as I was. But it took years of peeling back layers of conditioning and fear to understand that home wasn't something I had to earn or achieve—it was something I had to return to within myself.

The more I let go of the need to be something I wasn't, the more I embraced the idea that home is where I find peace in being me. Every step of my healing journey was a step toward this realization: that I already had everything I needed to feel at home. The answer wasn't out there—it was within me, waiting to be rediscovered.

The HOME Method as a Lifelong Practice

The HOME Method—Healing, Observing, Mindfulness, Embracing—has guided us throughout this journey, but it's not a one-time process. It's a practice you can return to throughout your life each time you feel lost, disconnected, or uncertain. These four steps will always help you find your way back home to yourself.

- **Healing:** Healing doesn't happen in a straight line. It unfolds in layers, often requiring us to revisit old wounds with deeper compassion. Each time you return to the healing process, you do so with more awareness and love for yourself.

- **Observing:** Self-awareness is key to coming home. By observing your thoughts, behaviors, and emotions, you create space for reflection and growth. This step is about cultivating curiosity and gentleness with yourself as you navigate life's changes.

- **Mindfulness:** Life will always have its ups and downs, but mindfulness helps you navigate these moments with presence and clarity. It allows you to return to the present moment, where you can make choices that align with your truest self.

- **Embracing:** Embracing is the culmination of this process—embracing yourself, your journey, your imperfections, and your growth. It's about accepting where you are and trusting that everything is unfolding as it should.

The Beauty of Imperfection and Ongoing Growth

One of the most important lessons along the way is that there is beauty in imperfection. So often, we pressure ourselves to have everything figured out to live up to impossible standards. But life isn't about being perfect—it's about being real, about growing through what you go through.

Coming home to yourself means embracing these imperfections. It means letting go of the need to have everything resolved and instead celebrating the process of becoming. Healing is never linear, and growth often comes in ways we don't expect. But through it all, you learn to be more compassionate with yourself, to see the value in your journey, and to recognize that this—exactly where you are—is part of the homecoming.

Living HOME in Every Aspect of Your Life

As you move forward, remember that the HOME Method is something you can bring into every part of your life. Whether it's in your relationships, your career, or your personal growth, you can always come back to these steps. They serve as a grounding force, a way to navigate life's complexities with more grace, self-compassion, and authenticity.

1. **Healing:** When you're faced with challenges or emotional pain, ask yourself what needs healing. Be kind to yourself in those moments, offering the same compassion you would give to someone you love.

2. **Observing:** Cultivate awareness in your daily life. Notice how your thoughts and actions align—or don't—with your true self. This gentle self-awareness is the foundation of authentic growth.

3. **Mindfulness:** Practice mindfulness in everything you do. Whether it's in conversations, work, or self-care, stay present and connected to what feels true for you in that moment.

4. **Embracing:** Embrace your journey with all its twists and turns. Trust that every experience, even the difficult ones, is leading you closer to your true self.

A Personal Invitation: Continue Coming Home

As you close this chapter, I invite you to carry this journey with you. Coming home to yourself is not something that happens just once—it's a continual practice of reconnecting with your truth, your heart, and your authentic self.

Every time you face a challenge, every time you feel lost, remember that you can always come home to yourself.

Story: My Ongoing Homecoming

Even now, after all the years of healing, self-discovery, and growth, I find myself coming home again and again. There are still moments when I feel disconnected or unsure when old fears resurface, or new challenges arise. But I no longer search outside of myself for the answers. Instead, I return to the HOME Method and the tools I've cultivated along the way.

Each time I come back to myself, I am reminded that home is not a place I need to search for—it's already within me. And with that realization comes peace. No matter where life takes me, no matter what changes or uncertainties arise, I know I am always able to return to the safe, loving, and grounded space inside of me. This is the true meaning of coming home.

Conclusion: You Have Arrived

As you step forward from this book and into the next chapter of your life, know that you have already found the home you were seeking. It's not somewhere out there—it's within you. You carry it with you, always.

Trust in your journey. Trust in your growth. Trust in the strength and wisdom you've gained along the way. And whenever you feel lost, disconnected, or unsure, know that you have everything you need to find your way back.

Welcome home!

Affirmations for Coming Home

Here are some affirmations to remind you of the journey home:

1. I am at home within myself.

2. I trust my journey, knowing that I am always growing and evolving.

3. I release the need for perfection and embrace my imperfections with love.

4. I am worthy of love, peace, and happiness just as I am.

5. I honor my healing process and give myself grace.

6. I am my own safe place.

7. I trust that I am exactly where I need to be at this moment.

8. I carry home within me wherever I go.

9. I live in alignment with my true self and embrace my authentic path.

10. I am always returning home to myself with love and compassion.

References and Suggestions for Continuous Reading and Practice

As you continue on your path of self-healing and growth, the following books, resources, and tools can further deepen your journey. Whether you're exploring mindfulness, trauma healing, self-compassion, or spiritual guidance, these references will provide valuable support as you practice the HOME Method and live authentically.

1. **Quantum Healing Hypnosis Technique (QHHT)**
   - **Summary:** QHHT is a form of hypnosis developed by Dolores Cannon that allows individuals to access their subconscious mind and past life memories to gain insights into healing and

personal growth. During a QHHT session, a trained practitioner guides you into a deep state of hypnosis, often known as the theta state, where you can connect with your higher self and past life experiences and receive messages that aid in healing and self-discovery.

- **Why It's Helpful:** QHHT can be a powerful tool for healing unresolved trauma, gaining clarity about your soul's purpose, and connecting with your higher self. This modality ties into the Healing and Embracing aspects of the HOME Method, as it provides a way to access deeper wisdom and let go of old patterns.

URL for more information: Official QHHT Website

2. **The Power of Now by Eckhart Tolle**

   - **Summary:** The Power of Now focuses on living in the present moment and freeing yourself from the mental chatter that causes suffering. Eckhart Tolle emphasizes mindfulness as the key to personal growth and spiritual awakening.

   - **Why It's Helpful:** This book complements the mindfulness aspect of the HOME Method by teaching you how to stay present, observe your thoughts, and release attachments to past and future worries.

   URL: The Power of Now on Amazon

3. **Healing the Shame That Binds You by John Bradshaw**

- **Summary:** In Healing the Shame That Binds You, John Bradshaw addresses the toxic shame that can develop from childhood trauma and unresolved emotional wounds. He provides strategies for healing these deep-seated feelings of inadequacy and worthlessness.
- **Why It's Helpful:** This book deeply resonates with the healing work discussed in the HOME Method, specifically in addressing childhood wounds and shame that might be holding you back from living authentically.

  URL: Healing the Shame That Binds You on Amazon

4. **The Drama of the Gifted Child by Alice Miller**

   - **Summary:** The Drama of the Gifted Child explores how early childhood trauma can shape our adult lives, particularly when children are forced to meet their parents' emotional needs rather than their own. Alice Miller emphasizes the importance of healing these early wounds for authentic living.
   - **Why It's Helpful:** This book sheds light on how unresolved childhood trauma influences adult behavior, helping you gain clarity as you work through the Healing and Observing aspects of the HOME Method.

     URL: The Drama of the Gifted Child on Amazon

5. **Playing the Matrix by Mike Dooley**

   - **Summary:** In Playing the Matrix, Mike Dooley offers a practical approach to manifesting your dreams by focusing on the "what" and letting go of the "how." The book teaches you to set clear intentions while trusting the universe to fill in the details.

Why It's Helpful: This book supports the Embracing aspect of the HOME Method by helping you release control over outcomes and trust in the process of life, encouraging a mindset of openness and flow.

URL: Playing the Matrix on Amazon

6. You Can Heal Your Life by Louise Hay

- **Summary:** Louise Hay's classic You Can Heal Your Life focuses on how thoughts, beliefs, and emotions affect physical and emotional well-being. She provides affirmations and practical exercises to help heal limiting beliefs and foster self-love.

- **Why It's Helpful:** This book ties into the Healing and Mindfulness aspects of the HOME Method by teaching how to shift negative thought patterns and heal yourself through positive affirmations and self-compassion.

  URL: You Can Heal Your Life on Amazon

7. Ask Your Guides by Sonia Choquette

- **Summary:** Ask Your Guides is a practical guide to connecting with your spiritual guides and higher self for guidance and clarity in life. Sonia Choquette teaches how to develop intuition and receive messages from the spiritual realm.

- **Why It's Helpful:** For those on a spiritual journey, this book offers tools to deepen your connection to your intuition and higher guidance, supporting the Observing and Embracing aspects of the HOME Method.

  URL: Ask Your Guides on Amazon

8. Insight Timer App

- **Summary:** Insight Timer is a free meditation app that provides thousands of guided meditations, mindfulness courses, and calming music to support meditation practices.

- **Why It's Helpful:** Mindfulness is essential to the HOME Method, and this app provides practical, daily tools to help you stay grounded, mindful, and connected to yourself.

  URL: Insight Timer App